How To Trade Options

A Step-by-Step Guide for Beginners

Richard Miller

TABLE OF CONTENTS

Introduction

Financial markets have taken the world by storm once again after their recovery from the crash of March 2020. After a correction of more than 3 months, the most famous index, the S&P 500 surpassed its previous all-time high.

A lot of people are now trying to improvise themselves as professional options traders and are losing a lot of money, only helping those who actually know what they are doing accumulate an incredible amount of wealth that will lead to generational fortunes.

To join the club of the few options traders that actually make it, you need the right strategies and the right mindset. Notice how we did not include a large initial capital. In fact, while having more money to trade means having more fire power, it is not necessary to have thousands of dollars to build wealth through options trading.

In fact, when we started options trading, we only had a few hundreds to put into the market, but that sum yielded us thousands and thousands of dollars over the span of a few years. The beauty of options trading is that it allows traders with little capital to use leverage and get bigger exposure. While this means more risk, it can also translate into bigger gains in a shorter period of time.

In this book you are going to discover all the strategies that have allowed us to take our options trading skills to the next level and everything that helped us understand financial markets. If you diligently apply our advice, we are sure you are going to see amazing results in a relatively short period of time, since the options market is offering an amazing number of opportunities.

Please, stay away from all the shiny objects of the market. Just focus on a few strategies, study them deeply and then milk the market like a cash cow. That is the real secret of market wizards!

To your success!

Chapter 1 - An Introduction to Trading Psychology

Trading psychology is a fundamental element, as one wrong move in trading can lead to losing a large capital. The psychology of the trader has always been a key element, since every trader carries out operations based on their past experiences and knowledge.

Operating on the markets is a very complex activity, also from the point of view of the emotional and cognitive aspects involved. Traders are in fact investing their savings and this carries a lot of stress on the trader.

By trading psychology we mean the trader's way of perceiving and responding to the market.

The way to act obviously depends on the experiences that the trader has had and on their past. Before starting to trade it is necessary to have a solid psychological preparation and Spartan discipline. In fact, emotions can play a fundamental role and you risk not making the right choice due to fear, stress, euphoria and so on.

Getting started with a demo account may be the way to go, although eventually every trader will go through their biggest challenge: the first big profit or the first big loss with real money.

It is on this occasion that traders discover firsthand how much psychology is a preponderant element in dealing with this activity.

Trading psychology can be the "extra mile" that distinguishes a good trader from an excellent one. You cannot therefore leave this aspect out and put it aside in your preparation, but you must be able to properly control your emotions.

In the next chapters we are going to discuss some key elements of trading psychology.

Chapter 2 - The Mind of the Successful Options Trader

This chapter comes from a reflection on my trading activity, which took place at a certain time. In fact, back then I was applying great energy to this activity but did not get the results I wanted. In my opinion this is a big fault because, if the purpose of trading is not fun but profit, the results must be enormous in percentage (3 digits per year must be the target).

By carrying out a sort of analysis of my work, looking for what could be the causes of this "failure", I was able to understand, from very interesting readings on the Internet, that psychological elements play an equally important role to those of the trader's predictive abilities. It is as important as money management strategies, choosing the right trading instruments, and every element described in this book.

It may happen that a trader, while making a series of small percentage but constant gains, systematically gives up a large part of these gains with a single operation. Or after a profitable period, they collect a series of huge losses, one after the other.

The trader's psychological attitude influences the success of the operation on the one hand, but the vice versa also tends to be true. Therefore, trading operations can, but should not, influence the psychological state of the trader. The biggest problem is summed up by the concept of expectation. Let's quickly list the psychological attitudes that a losing dynamic can generate in a trader whose psychic state is deteriorating in the face of repeated losses.

At the operational level:

- Trading against the market
- Irrational trading

- Revenge trading on a financial instrument, perhaps with a higher capital
- Assimilation to gambling
- Total financial loss

On a psychological level:

- Stress
- Fear of making mistakes
- Performance anxiety
- Loss of self-esteem
- Ache
- Superstition, especially on dates
- Wrong perception of money
- Wrong perception of risk
- Distortion of reality and cognitive dissonance
- Instability
- Negative attitudes to life
- Loss of concentration
- Crying, loss of control and anger, or madness

- Suicide

We concluded the psychological list with suicide, and the operational list with total financial loss: they are realities that need to be paid close attention.

The attitudes, the warning signs of a losing trader materialize in various points:

- You do not use a trading system, perhaps simply because you do not want to use it: the key element, beyond the predictive capacity, is precisely the methodology and diligence
- Lack of purpose
- Attempt to win money instead of placing a trade
- Lack of patience, control, or strategy

The origin of the problem, for a capable person, and of all the possible negatives that can be imagined, arise exactly when the trader has placed an expectation on the trading decision. Precisely that element, if the outcome of the decision is wrong, produces:

- Emotional pain
- Negative psychological impact
- Engagement of a losing trader attitude.

And this even in cases where the decision taken has led to a success of the operation. Perhaps because the trader could have been imagining to obtain a superior result, and therefore seeing the «glass half empty».

If the outcome of the decision is not wrong, it produces the expectation of adverse effects but which, although positive, can also lead to negative effects with exaltation, narcissism, wrong perception of the risk that therefore brings you back to a losing trader.

The problem with all this is precisely the

expectation. Good or bad that goes, it ends badly anyway. On the other hand, the positive trader, winning, is the one who manifests themselves with concepts that mirror these listed. Try them in mind on the previous list. Only one probably remains unchanged, stress is always there.

What is the origin of a winning trader at this point? Well it seems the discovery of hot water but it is the Trading Plan. The trading plan is an investment and action project that is very often done when markets are closed, away from the emotions of the battlefield. The feeling of pleasure is associated with having thought, implemented and respected the trading plan, not only when you make a profit. Only in this way, losses can be accepted as an ineliminable part of trading.

Sometimes nervousness can be anything but small and grows with the increase in the sum dedicated to the trade. Some people by nature manage to be less emotional than others even with large sums, but in the initial moments of this activity most traders will be subjected to mental and emotional stress.

The causes of this stress are many and the most common are not having a well-defined method, being unsure of the way of operating on the market and getting caught up in emotion. As we have seen, in fact, emotions are the trader's worst enemy.

When our trade goes wrong we will be affected by nervousness and other feelings which will increase the amount of stress we can bear. If you then add the hours of study, the hours of market observation and the lost trades, the situation really starts to be difficult to manage.

These are those moments that almost all traders go through when starting this business, sadly accompanied by a loss of money on the market.

How to cope with stressful situations

First of all we have to manage everything related to trading in a programmed way, from observation to operational hours.

If we have opened a real account and have been trading for two months, we do not use our capital until we have an operating method. We observe the market movements on what they want to be our reference financial instruments and timeframes.

We can safely work on a Demo Account, in order to cancel the emotional factor that at the moment would only be an enemy. What matters to us now is having a method, then thinking about being profitable. This demo period should be at least 6 months long.

I imagine that many of you will have turned up their noses because it seems to be a very long time but you have to be very patient and feel confident before operating correctly on the market.

When we have a valid trading plan or in any case the knowledge that allows us to control our emotions, we will be able to manage the stress of online trading much better. Another thing of fundamental importance is to dedicate the right hours to rest at night, in order to always be energetic and careful in dealing with the situations of observation and study of the markets.

When you start to feel tired, it is good to take small breaks of a few days because working in suboptimal conditions will not lead to anything, if not to further complicate the situation.

The market is always there for you, so there is no reason to learn quickly.

Chapter 3 - Keeping Emotions Under Control

In trading it is very easy to get lost. Most traders, by logging into their platform to try to earn a few pips, generally tend to forget the basic rules of good risk management.

Here are five questions we should ask ourselves, if we don't want bad habits to cost us more than they should.

Have I checked my trades?

Online trading makes it very simple to execute trades, but for this very reason it is also very easy to make mistakes. Despite having a winning trading plan, it would be completely useless if the mistake was precisely the "typing" of the order itself!

Checking what we have written more than once can save us from one 0 too many.

Do I have a plan?

Trading is not an impulsive activity and always requires a plan.

There are traders who trade completely on emotion and enter trades irrationally, without ever thinking fully. At the very least, we should have a plan to get in or out of our positions. In this way, we will be able to limit the disastrous emotional reactions, due to any unfavorable price trend.

Can I take profit on winning trades?

Another often forgotten trading practice is to collect part of the profits when the price action is still favorable.

When the wind is in your favor it is very tempting to continue riding the trend with the full position. But by doing so we expose ourselves to potential volatility. Keeping part of the position out, on the other hand, limits the risk. After all, the saying "the trend is your friend, until it ends" is certainly not a coincidence.

Do I deserve a break?

Do you feel overwhelmed by your trades? Are your fundamental and technical analyzes often wrong (more than you admit)?

If the answer is yes to any of these questions, then it's time to consider taking a break from trading.

Getting away from the markets completely, avoiding emotional involvement with any type of position, allows you to restore the ability to analyze and see the themes and issues of the market from another perspective.

Sometimes, it is just a pause that allows us to understand the mistakes of the past and how to correct them. Maintaining your mental clarity must always be the first rule of any trading and risk management strategy.

How much do I have in the account?

Although it is pleasant to leave the trading account with the amount of money that allows us a "little freedom", leaving there too much can lead to impulsive and hasty decisions, such as opening positions that are too large for our reach or to over-trading, in which you go on to the bitter end on the market, without perhaps realizing that you are losing everything.

Withdrawing money can be a good habit. Among other things, being a very profitable traer requires attention to the process and not just to profits.

Every so often, therefore, it is good to switch off and take a vacation from the markets, go shopping and so on, enjoying the hard-earned fruits of your work.

Chapter 4 - Setting Trading Goals

Awareness of oneself and one's abilities (including financial ones) is one of the fundamental prerequisites for a trading activity that is not only profitable, but also gives satisfaction on a personal level.

"There is no favorable wind for the sailor who does not know where to go", said Seneca.

How do you see yourselves in one year? What are the goals that you set for yourself and that you have respected this year?

In trading these points are very important, since we must understand which trade has brought the most benefits and how it has affected our capital.

Setting the goal of transforming 1,000 dollars into 100,000 is perhaps exaggerated, moreover, I can't be the one to tell you how and how much to invest, also because I don't know you. The only thing I can do is show you one of the possible paths to set goals that are concrete and tailored to you.

Remember that goals must not only be set, but also respected. This is why it is important that they are trader-friendly projects, sustainable and above all possible to achieve.

It all starts with self awareness

The first thing you need to do is look in the mirror and ask yourself specific questions, answering them in an equally precise manner. There is only you and your self awareness, you cannot lie to yourself. So start trying the following questions and answering them precisely:

- Where am I in my trading career?
- What is my average monthly earnings?
- How much do I lose on average in a month?

- How long does it take to recover the losses?
- What are my strengths as a trader?
- What are my weaknesses?
- Have I tested my trading system (or philosophy) accurately enough to determine its potential duration?

There are almost certainly plenty of other questions to ask yourself once in front of the mirror, but these can be a good starting point for a (difficult, it must be said) moment of introspection.

In fact, you have to test yourself by asking concrete questions about your expectations.

For example:

- How many profits have been on my account during the last month. And in the last 3 months, and 6 months?
- How many hours a day do I spend on average in front of the markets, and how many in a

week?

- How much money can I risk (with one account and for each single trade)?
- At this point the analysis must become more in-depth and we must ask ourselves: how do I intend to manage the risk?

Once all these ideas and reflections have been written down, only then can we start talking about goals. Once again, the goals are entirely personal and we can only speak broadly here.

What are your goals?

Do your goals have a purpose or do they follow a progression? I mean, do you have a target (let's say 12 months) to reach? Or is your goal to progressively increase profits? Do you want to make trading your main source of income, or is it a way to make (or lose) some extra money at the end of the month?

There is never a correct answer to these

questions: it all depends only on you. It depends on how much you want to earn in a year with trading, which stocks you want to bet on and above all how much you want to bet on the market.

Chapter 5 - Money Lessons from Napoleon Hill and Benjamin Graham

Napoleon Hill in his book "Think and Grow Rich" explains in a simple and effective way what is the psychology of money, while Benjamin Graham when he wrote "The intelligent investor" defined the essence of investing in the stock market.

These two books are the basis of everything you need to know about the psychology of trading, which is also the psychology of money. Why? because it is in the mind that everything moves and it is money that manages this movement.

It is always useful to start from a solid psychological foundation in addressing your training path in trading. The books by Napoleon Hill and Benjamin Graham are really two excellent starting points to do so.

So, don't just think about trading but already broaden your views by assimilating the information you need to become a successful trader. There are no foolproof guides to trading but there are strategic guides to become rich.

To get to the idea of trading options, there must have been something or someone that prompted you to consider the possibility or at least to really try. When you know what you want to do, the rest comes by itself.

Do not delude yourself that you are rich, intelligent and invincible about everything you do, but be concrete, realistic and very self-critical; Visualize the goal to be achieved, whatever it is without limits of size, and insert places, people, scenography, soundtrack and objects in your image and always keep this vision alive.

Answer the five Ws, namely Who (who), What (what), When (when), Where (where), Why (why), which are used in journalism: give yourself clear and sensible answers about your intention and write them down. Here too try to always have with you the sheet where you have pinned these thoughts.

Always re-read the two books provided above, "Think & Grow Rich" and "The Intelligent Investor" which will help you even and above all in difficult moments. Expect from yourself great determination and perseverance to work every day and improve your knowledge.

Observe and try to understand every movement you see, from yours, to others, so in addition to technical analysis, focus on psychological analysis of yourself and those around you.

See options trading as a happy job that enriches you first of all internally and then also in your pockets. If you bet too much on just the thought of getting rich, this will never happen. So try to visualize also the path to get to wealth and the results will be different. Find your own style and your own way of analyzing, evaluating, thinking and behaving, because only in this way will you be able to move well in your work. Listen to suggestions and advice but do not imitate them too much. You do you.

Do not fear losses, because it is from the losses that the best wins are fueled and in this case the gains. If you lose money, try to understand why this happened and vice versa.

Have fun responsibly, so dare beyond the limits you can afford. Every tradejust has to be an intelligent action, even in the event of a loss. If you enjoy what you do, the same passion will lead you to success and enthusiasm.

Chapter 6 - Before Thinking About Becoming a Professional Trader

The prospect of becoming an options trader is very interesting indeed.

You would be your own boss, the payback is potentially very high and, above all, it is something you like. What more could you want?

But - don't forget - options trading is serious business. In addition to being able to make a lot of money quickly, there are many risks that play their part. Becoming a full-time options trader, relying only on trading for all your daily expenses, is easier said than done.

If you haven't done so yet, you can open a completely free demo account with one of the trading platforms of your choice and start training.

Before you even begin to consider going pro, here are 4 questions you should ask yourself.

Are you successful with options trading at the moment?

Don't think that by hanging up your work suit and starting trading in your pajamas 24/7, you will have enough time to make the right trading decisions, because you won't. If you are not making money now that you are a part-time trader, your account is unlikely to grow with full-time trading.

You need to be sure you have some discipline, without doubting yourself in the slightest. You need to keep a trading journal and do your homework. If you are not doing them now, why do you think you are going to do them later?

Are you mentally strong enough?

Okay, trading doesn't put that much pressure on you today. But can you imagine how much pressure you would have if your options trading activity depended on paying your mortgage payment?

The pressure that comes from being a full-time trader can potentially lead to being a bad trader. It would put you in a vulnerable position where it is difficult to control emotions and you could make bad choices that you wouldn't normally make.

Do you have enough money?

Of course, capital is an important issue to consider when choosing to enter and remain in the world of forex full time. Make sure you have enough money to take risks and are comfortable with the fluctuations that will come.

And most importantly, be prepared for the eventual arrival of a losing streak or a sharp decline in your account.

Full time options trading can work if you are able to accept that your account can fluctuate with the market. Don't rely solely on your trading profits to cover ongoing expenses.

We recommend that you always consider worst-case scenarios, such as a few consecutive months of loss, before staying in the market full time.

If you think you're not comfortable with undercapitalization and big losses, you should reconsider your chances of success in full-time options trading. The constant pressure of having to keep your profits intact could hurt you if you are not ready to face the consequences.

Why do you want to be a full-time trader?

You need to be clear on the reasons why you want to become a full-time trader.

Do you really think it's for you? Or do you just want to get rich fast? Is it just because you hate your job so much that you are looking around for an alternative?

It is crucial to have an honest assessment of your current situation, your skills as a trader, your mental stamina, your economic possibilities.

If you rely mostly on salary to pay your bills, mortgage, or school fees, full-time options trading may not be for you yet. You don't want to jeopardize your lifestyle or put your family's well-being on the line and be under constant pressure to make money.

Once again: options trading is a serious business - there are a lot of risks involved and it's not just your money. Take time first to trade options part-time and make sure you are financially, mentally and emotionally ready.

Chapter 7 - The Importance of the Demo Account

Like all fashions, trading also attracts thousands of newbies around the world every day attracted by rumors of easy money, potentially brilliant intuitions or more often naive illusions.

However, trading is an activity that has at least 3 critical points:

- It is complex.
- It can generate addiction and severe stress.
- It puts the money of those who practice it at risk.

Above all, the last point, of course, is decisive in evaluating the opportunity to embark on an activity of this kind, which can give a lot in terms of emotions and satisfaction, but in the same way (and perhaps for the same reasons) it can ruin and destroy a person.

Even if the adrenaline of being on the market is very often the real "service" that the trader pays by losing their money, it is also true that the risks of addiction should push anyone to consider very carefully the opportunity to start options trading.

The right result of such an assessment should be the following: if I want to trade I have to give up the emotions it can give me. I have to learn to be cold and to operate in an orderly and disciplined way, almost as if I were a thinking machine.

How do you get there? With a very slow and gradual path that starts with the use of demo accounts and ends with real money trading little by little, always with the willingness to stop and take a step back.

Chapter 8 - More on Trading Psychology

To be successful in online Forex and CFD trading, a trader must demonstrate a lot of skills and develop a lot of skills. Among these: understanding the basic principles of trading, fundamental analysis, markets, etc. A fundamental element, to say the least, is the psychology of trading.

Even if this is not a true academic study, the right psychological approach to the subject is able to turn a trader's experience towards success or failure. When starting to operate in the world of online trading, traders develop strategies trying to make as much profit as possible. Knowing how to manage one's emotions while maintaining the right amount of discipline in one's business is an equally necessary skill.

Trading never stops

One moment you are profitable, the next

moment you are at a loss. It takes presence, always and in any case. In the world of trading, one learns to make quick decisions. The moves must be considered from the outset. Sticking to the initial plan without venturing into risky maneuvers when in trouble is the best way to make balanced choices. In other words, leave your emotions outside trading. In any case, it is useless to think of getting by without doubts that they cross our brain. As a trader, be prepared to confront all your emotionality.

Trading and emotions

Emotions in trading can lead to evaluation errors with inevitable money losses, so here are the most common feelings experienced by traders.

Fear

When trading, fear is probably the first emotion you get when you start seeing charts, screens and information that you can't understand. This is all a terrible feeling indeed. You may even wish you would want to run away by running for the hills to avoid investing and feel safe, however by doing so you will lose potential gains. Fear can be a limiting factor causing the failure to open potentially profitable positions, so here is the importance of correctly calculating the risks in trading.

Understanding the fear that lurks inside you is the first step to overcome your emotions, a feeling that can make you pull back just because you are starting to grapple with something you still know little about. However, trading is not a threat. There is little to fear when trading. What it takes is simply time and knowledge to understand what you are doing, why you are doing it, and how you can benefit from all of this.

Greed

Greed can be your worst enemy. In order not to be overwhelmed, you need to know when it's time to leave the field and pocket the profits. Experienced traders would never want to log out when trading is going well. But this mentality can be your undoing.

Markets are not for people who believe in sensations, and changes, dictated by specific elements, are on the agenda. Overcoming a hard blow is never easy, but defeating greed will be even more difficult. Successfully concluding a trading operation does not guarantee that the next one will have the same outcome, so exit the position and enjoy your profit.

It is very important to recognize as soon as possible "the warning bells of greed", decide that you do not have to "do a little more" and stick to your trading plan on which you have already based your initial decision after careful reasoning and evaluations techniques. Greed can lead to excessive trading, a condition very similar to gambling addiction that must absolutely be avoided.

Hope

In trading, hope is a rather useless emotion. Even if all traders experience it, it can be quite damaging. Thinking positive for a trader is important, but optimism must still be kept in check by confronting reality on a daily basis. Traders often fall into the trap of creating a false sense of hope that the markets will adjust to their expectations, saving their positions. This is a textbook example of the wrong approach to trading.

Regret

From fear to panic, there is anger pushing traders to regret losing a good deal. You may therefore be tempted to enter the same "missed" trade with the hope of making a profit but on which you have already arrived too late and thus incurring an inevitable loss. Excitement and regret can both be dangerous to experience during the decision-making process. Regret can turn into demotivation after a series of failed trades, gradually slipping into frustration and finally saying goodbye forever to the world of online trading. The solution is to maintain discipline in one's business and judgment. This is exactly what successful traders have done and do and is what you will have to strive for.

Chapter 9 - Money Management 101

Money management is one of the fundamental factors for building a winning trading strategy, even more so in situations where high leverage is used, as often happens in options trading.

The rules of money management are mostly common sense indications which, however, are not always followed in daily operations by most private traders.

So let's see the main rules to be adopted for the correct management and allocation of the capital to be invested.

- Don't be undercapitalized. It is important to have adequate capital for the instrument on which we are going to operate and not to take excessive risks. These two principles help you survive long enough to be able to thrive. There are numerous examples of traders with small capital who were "eliminated" quickly at the beginning of their career.

- Risk, in a single transaction, only a small percentage of the available capital, preferably no more than 2% of your portfolio. You can build up fortunes in the long run even by trading only 2-3 contracts at a time. The important thing is to survive long enough to continue working on the market, without being wiped out.

- Use stop-losses. Enter them immediately after taking a position on the market. "Mental" stop-losses don't work. Keep the maximum draw-down low (20-25%).

- Limit the risk of your entire portfolio to a maximum of 20%. In other words, if you were to suffer stop-loss at the same time in all the positions you had taken, make sure that 80% of the starting capital still remains.

- Maintain a risk/reward ratio to a minimum of 1: 2 and preferably 1: 3 or more. In other words, for every pip away from the stop loss, aim for 2 or 3 pips for the take profit.

- Never add positions to positions that are at a loss. In other words, do not average down. If you find yourself on the wrong side of the market, admit it quickly and close the position. Your ego is often detrimental to proper trading.

- Try to lock at least part of the profits you are making. If you are lucky enough to take a substantial move in a short time, liquidate at least part of the position (by moving the stop loss into positive territory for example).

When you have suffered a series of consecutive losses, stop and re-evaluate the market and your working methodology. The market will always be there waiting for you. Gann summarizes the concept in his book "How to make profits in commodities", published more than 50 years ago. "When you make a series of consecutive losses, whether small or large, there is something wrong with you, and not with the market. The trend may have changed. My rule is to go out and wait. Study the reason for the losses. Remember that you will never lose money by being out of the market".

Chapter 10 - The Kelly Criterion

We often hear about the importance of diversification, risk management, and money management.

How much money do we have to put into a trade? What percentage of our portfolio can we allocate to a single stock? When should we sell or buy? These are all questions we can answer by defining and trying to apply a money management system.

In this chapter we address the Kelly Criterion, one of the many techniques that can be used to manage your money efficiently.

History of the Kelly Criterion

John Kelly, who worked for the Bell Laboratory at AT&T, originally developed the formula by which he is known to study signal noise problems that arise in long distance phone calls. Immediately after the method was published, however, the community of professional betters realized the potential that the method expressed when applied to the study of betting optimization (bet sizing) on horse racing.

The system allowed players to maximize the bet by optimizing it for the long run. Currently, the Kelly Formula is used by many as a money management system not only in gambling but also in investment activities.

The basics of the Kelly Criterion

There are two fundamental components that make up the Kelly Criterion:

- The winning probability or the probability, that each single operation (trade) translates into a positive result (gain)
- Average win / average loss ratio (winAv / lossAv ratio) or the average value of the transactions closed in winning (average of the gain) divided by the average value of the transactions

closed at a loss (average of the loss)

These two factors are inserted into the Kelly equation:

Kelly% = W - (1 - W) / R

where:

- W = Winning probability
- R = WinAverage / lossAverage ratio

The result is the "Kelly percentage" (Kelly%), which we will examine very soon.

How to put it into practice

The Kelly system can be implemented by following these simple steps.

- Record your last 50-60 trades on the market. Take the list of transactions made with your broker or, if you are using a mechanical trading system, you can carry out a back testing of the same and record the values obtained.

- Calculate the "W", i.e. the odds of winning. To do this, divide the number of trades that generated a gain by the total trades made (positive and negative). The result will be a number between 0 and 1 (example: 50 total operations. 30 closed in gain and 20 closed in loss. W = 30/50 = 0.6).

- Calculate "R", i.e. the "winAv / lossAv" ratio. To do this, divide the average value of the gain generated by positive operations by the average value of the losses. (for example: average of transactions in gain = $500; average of transactions closed in loss = $300; R = 500/300 = 1.66).
- Insert the obtained W and R values into the Kelly equation K% = W - (1 - W) / R.
- Mark the result obtained.

Interpretation of results

The formula produces as a result a number less than 1. It represents the size of the position that should be taken on the market; the percentage of your portfolio, that is, with which you should perform the operation.

For example, if the result of the equation were 0.05, then you should use 5% of your portfolio for every single position you take on the market. This system, in essence, tells you how much you should "diversify".

The system also requires practical sense. A rule of thumb to keep in mind, regardless of what it might turn out to be applying your statistics to the Kelly formula, is never to put more than 20-25% of your capital in a single trade. A position above this percentage would be too high a risk for anyone in the long run.

The efficiency of the system

Kelly's system is based on the application of a mathematical formula but some may wonder if a system developed to study "noise" phenomena on telephone lines could also be suitable for the options market.

By showing the simulated growth of a "trading account" based on a mathematical model, its reliability can be demonstrated. Necessarily, the two required variables must be entered correctly and it is based on the assumption that the investor keeps the risk parameters (variables) assumed originally fixed.

Here is an example.

Simulated trend over time of 30 trading accounts with the parameters indicated on the right.

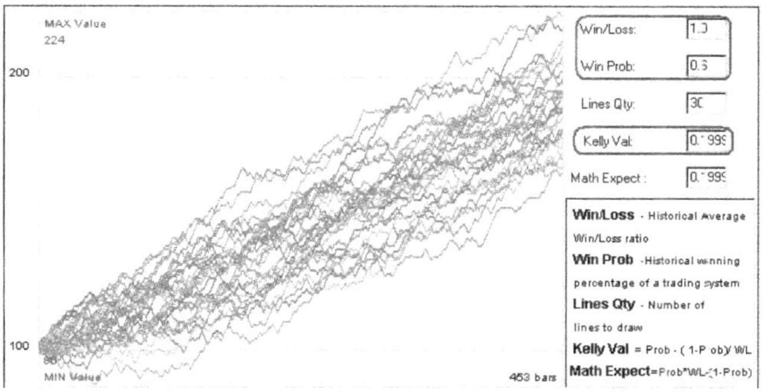

In the image above we can see the simulated trend of 30 "trading accounts", out of 453 transactions, through the representation of their "equity curve". Origin of the simulation on the value 100.

The parameters adopted are:

- the average of the single loss equal to the average of the single gain (win / loss = 1)
- the probability of a winning trade equal to 60% (win prob = 0.6)

The Kelly Criterion suggests, in this example,

to allocate no more than 19.9% of the available capital (bet-size) to carry out each operation (therefore a maximum of 5 operations on different instruments at the same time).

The result shown in the image is a long-term positive return on all the "accounts" of the 30 traders in the example (note, however, some negative returns in the short term with a minimum of 86, which corresponds to 14% of loss). The maximum simulated «return», at the end of the 453 operations, was 124% (start at 100, end at 224).

No money management system is perfect. This system helps you diversify your portfolio efficiently, but there are many things the system cannot do. For instance, it cannot select the winning trades on your behalf; it cannot assure you that you will continue trading with the same parameters as now (win / loss ratio and winning probability), and it cannot predict sudden market crashes.

Furthermore, there is always a certain level of "luck" or randomness in the market that can alter your "ideal" performance. For example, consider again the image above. It is clear that the best simulated "return" was 124% but the worst was about 50%. Both accounts had the same initial parameters, but the "randomness" in the succession of losses and gains can create temporary fluctuations in the values of the accounts themselves.

Money management cannot assure you that you will always get staggering positive returns from your trades, but it can help you limit and contain losses and optimize and maximize gains through efficient portfolio diversification.

Kelly's Criterion is one of many models that can be used to help you do this and it is the one I recommend you.

Chapter 11 - The Importance of Money Management

Talking about money management for the options market is a bit like talking about aerodynamics and Formula 1.

Money management is very important to make you earn in the options market as much as an aerodynamic single seater allows a driver to win a race.

As we have seen, by the term "money management" we mean the set of fundamental rules for making money with options in the long term.

Here are the best tips for proper money management.

Always use stop loss and take profit

These two points are very important for the correct management of each individual position. The stop loss is the point where you decide to automatically stop a loss of money while the take profit is the point where a profitable position is closed to collect the profit.

The use of the stop loss is particularly difficult, especially for new traders, due to the fact that they do not accept to lose money.

In reality, the options market is made up of gains and losses (even the largest investors lose), so you simply have to resign yourself, sometimes, to losing from an open position, understand where you went wrong and re-enter the market with new strength.

Never risk too much

Brokers make available to traders levers that reach up to 500: 1. In other words, it means that with 1 dollar you can control 500 dollars.

This means that, with an account of 100 dollars, you can manage up to 500,000 dollars.

While this is tempting to the options trader

because the gains can be very large in proportion to the investment made, on the other hand it is too risky a choice to invest with too much leverage.

Remember that leverage affects your gains, but also your losses.

Good money management is also based on risk control.

Trading should be done on data, not feelings

Often novice traders open positions because "I think the euro can go up" or because "in my opinion the dollar will go down". There is nothing more wrong: options are a financial market, not a roulette wheel.

Choosing whether to enter the market and do it in one direction rather than the other must be a choice that is the result of the study and analysis of the market, not of sensations.

To sum this up, money management is very

important to be successful in options trading, without it you cannot legitimately expect to earn money in the long term and become a successful trader.

Chapter 12 - The Martingale Strategy

The theory behind the Martingale strategy turns out to be quite simple. It is a negative progression system, that is, which involves increasing the size of the position after a loss. In particular, the Martingale strategy involves doubling the size of the position when a loss is recorded.

The classic scenario of this system is the one that occurs when trying to change a result when there is a 50% chance that it will occur. This scenario has no expectations. You expect to do nothing and lose nothing in the long run. For this type of 50/50 system there are two schools of thought on how to decide the size of our position. The first, namely the Martingale strategy, argues that we must double the size of the position when we lose, in this way we will recover what was lost and achieve the performance we had set for ourselves.

The second school, the strategy against the Martingale, argues that position size should only be increased when profits are made.

Heads or tails

Imagine an investment that can only have two outcomes. In particular, they are both equally likely to occur. We call these results A and B. In commercial terms the risk / reward ratio is 1: 1. Suppose you decide to trade a total of $5 in the hope that the desired outcome - A - occurs. However, what results B ultimately occurs and you lose your investment.

For the next position, according to the Martingale method, it is necessary to increase the size to $10, trusting once again that the result A will occur. If B is repeated one more time, then the $10 will be lost.

Again, according to the Martingale strategy, you will need to double the size of your position and trade with $20 waiting for A to occur this time to make a profit. The technique then consists of repeating this operation until A occurs, which will cause the size of the winning position to exceed the sum of all previously accumulated losses.

Some possible sequences would be the following:

- Win in the first position and gain 5 dollars
- You lose in the first operation and win in the second. In this case, you lose 5 dollars in the first and receive 10 dollars in the second operation. The total profit would be $5.
- You lose in the first two positions and win in the third. In this case you lose $5 in the first operation, $10 in the second and win $20 in the third. The final gain would be $5.
- You lose in the first three operations and win in the fourth. So you will lose $5 in the first position, $10 in the second, $20 in the third and finally you will win $40 in the fourth. Again, the final

profit will be $5, after recovering all accumulated losses.

As you can see with these sequences and in all of these scenarios, when you win a position with Martingale trading you get more profit than losses, which in theory sounds very good. The problem, however, is that to do this, you have to risk more and more to make a small profit.

In our previous example, we only won $5 but with a losing streak of only three trades we are already risking $40. Imagine if this losing streak went on a little longer.

If you lose six consecutive times, in the previous case, you would risk $320 to get only $5 of profit. In other words, you risk a loss of $315 if you try to earn only $5. The odds of hitting a losing streak out of six trades are low but not insane. In fact, they exceed 1 percent.

What if your capital was 200 dollars in total? You would be forced to give up with a big loss in your pocket. This is a fundamental problem that distinguishes the Martingale strategy. Your chances of winning are only guaranteed if you have enough funds to keep doubling indefinitely.

This is usually not the case. The most common thing is that all traders have a limited capital to put at risk. The longer the Martingale method is applied, the greater the chances of a long streak of losses occurring.

In the next few pages, we will explain how a Martingale strategy works and see a practical example. For instance, the result of a Forex trade is variable because we can define the price level at which we collect profits or reduce our losses. In this way, we establish our potential earnings as a fixed amount.

The image below shows a one-minute chart of

the EURUSD pair with the RSI indicator. The RSI indicator will give us the entry point and help us to know the state of the market: if the RSI falls below 30, what it suggests is that there is over-selling. If, on the other hand, it exceeds 70, an excess of purchases will be estimated.

The chart shows that on April 16 at 14.58 the RSI (bottom, blue) is above line 70, which will mark our entry line.

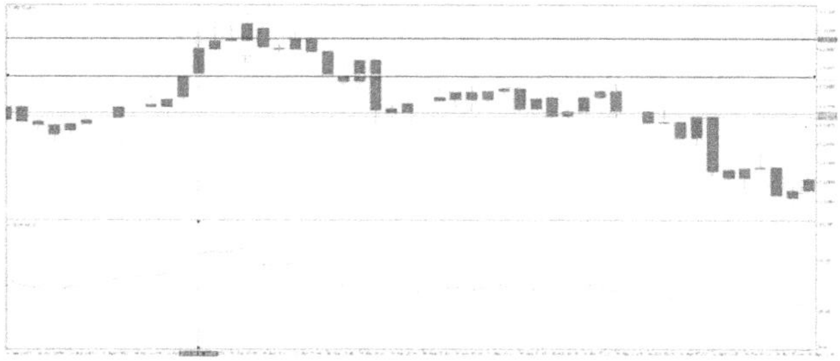

We are selling one lot of EURUSD at 1.13063 and setting the profit 30 pips below 1.13033. In case the market is in our favor, this will be the take profit point.

Our stop loss will be mentally set 30 pips

higher at 1.13093.

If the EURUSD continues to rise after our mental stop, we will lose at that point. The Martingale strategy invites us to double the risk in the next position. Therefore, we only use a mental stop loss instead of a real stop.

Why do this? Because it would make no sense to close one position and reopen another one twice as large.

We replace our initial take profit order with a new order to close both trades. The new take profit will be 30 pips below our new trade at 1.13063. In the first position we sold at 1.13063 and in the second position at 1.13093. The RSI will give us a new entry point and we will follow the same sequence again.

This is a very simple example to give you an idea of how the Martingale method would be applied to trading. As we have already said before, this system is very risky because we can chain together several lost positions in a row, even more so in a trending market.

The main drawback of the Martingale trading strategy is that it plays with its losses, which is generally considered to be a break with the rules of good money management. It is interesting to compare it with the reverse Martingale or anti-martingale strategy (a method often used by traders who follow the trend).

Chapter 13 - The Anti Martingale Strategy

We generally believe it is correct to consider the size of a trade independent of market parameters. It is frequent to build a trading system with sizes linked to price volatility. Low volatility, larger sizes and vice versa. Linking the size to market parameters can impact the equity line by not allowing you to correctly evaluate the trading strategy. Sizes that change according to market parameters will put more stress on the problems of overfitting of trading systems. We don't like this logic. In reality, even if today the financial instrument analyzed shows a low volatility, who assures us that tomorrow it will not increase?

How can the size of an operation be managed? The pillars that the trader must protect are their economic capital and psychological capital. The size of the operations must guarantee the safeguarding of both. One size management approach that we like is the anti-martingale strategy.

Martingale and trading

The martingale is a doubling betting system. As we have seen, this system provides for the doubling of the size invested for each transaction closed in loss. Proponents of this approach argue that through this methodology it is possible to cancel all losses with each successful trade. This system is generally used in the world of betting and gambling. In trading it is not possible to know precisely the probability of closing a trade in gain (unlike gambling such as throwing dice, roulette, etc.). Therefore, it is not possible to hypothesize with the study of probabilities how many consecutive loss transactions could be. Consecutive losses could also erode the entire economic capital (unless you have infinite capital and are willing to risk it all).

Furthermore, the losses (always increasing in line with the size) would also tend to erode the psychological capital, with all the resulting disadvantages.

Anti Martingale in trading

The anti-martingale method is the opposite of the martingale. When gaining transactions are closed, and therefore an increase in economic capital is recorded, it is possible to increase the size. On the contrary, when a transaction is recorded at a loss, and therefore the capital is reduced, the size is reduced. This method allows you to risk more when increasing capital and less when it is reduced. In our opinion, this methodology allows you to manage trading with greater control, offering numerous advantages from a psychological point of view.

Anti Martingale example in trading

For educational purposes we show you a very simplified example of capital management in trading with the anti-martingale method. Let's assume a trading strategy with take profit and stop loss at 4%. Let's assume that the percentage change in capital in the anti-Martingale is 50%. This means that for each loss operation the size will decrease by 50%, while it will increase by the same percentage for each gain operation. Obviously the decision of this percentage will significantly impact the trading results through the size management method with anti-martingale.

In our opinion, the anti-martingale, understood as doubling the capital every time winning operations are closed, is a wrong approach. In fact, a closing in loss would be enough to lose the gains of all trades made. There is no mathematical formula of position sizing that allows you to get rich. Position sizing allows you to manage the risk/reward ratio. The perception of risk cannot be measured objectively as it changes from person to person depending on many factors. Psychology is a fundamental element of trading, you should only take risks that allow you to work in your comfort zone. Your goal is to create a risk management strategy tailored to your skin. Without looking for complex mathematical formulas, our advice is to follow the basic logic of the anti-martingale, that is, to slightly increase the risks when things go well and reduce them when they go bad.

Chapter 14 - Larry William's Formula

Money management consists of two fundamental and inseparable areas: risk management and position sizing. The first analyzes the risk associated with the position taken on the market; the second identifies the capital to be invested in each single operation open on the market and the distribution of the capital among the various portfolio assets.

Proper risk management has the sole purpose of maximizing profit and minimizing losses, regardless of the trading system used. Each money management strategy follows a basic logic, consisting of several fundamental points:

- Availability of adequate capital for the financial instrument used;
- Risk limited to no more than 2-3% of the portfolio for each individual transaction;

- Use of the stop-loss after taking a position on the market;
- Definition of the maximum risk for the portfolio (drawdown): if all the stop-losses set are triggered at the same time, the trader must keep a sufficient share of capital to continue operating on the market;
- Quantifying the risk through a correct calculation of the risk / reward: for each risk unit, a target of 2-3 return units must be calculated;
- In-depth knowledge of the market in which you intend to invest;
- The outcome of each operation must be considered independently from that of the previous operation;
- Closing of part of the open positions in case of profit.

Among the optimization models of "position sizing" we can mention the Kelly Formula and the Larry Williams Formula.

As we have seen in a previous chapter, Kelly's formula has been used by gamblers to maximize bets by optimizing them in the long run. Subsequently, the scope of application of the model was extended to investment activities to calculate the share of capital to be used in each individual operation (F), given the available asset.

$$F = W - (1-W) / R$$

Where, W is the probability that each single trade results in a positive result. It is obtained by dividing the number of operations that generated a profit by the total number of operations carried out (positive and negative); R is the ratio of winning trades to losing trades, i.e. the average value of the trades closed in profit (average of earnings) divided by the average value of trades closed at a loss (average of losses).

The equation results in a number less than 1

which represents the size of the position that should be taken on the market, or the percentage of the portfolio to be allocated in each individual transaction. However, Kelly's formula neglects important evaluation parameters such as the drawdown of the system, the number of losing trades and the volatility of the market.

The Larry Williams formula represents an evolution of the Kelly formula and calculates the number of contracts / shares for the position to be taken on the market as a function of the risk percentage. This parameter is random since the average risk tolerance is a subjective parameter, so by changing this parameter the results generated by the system will be different.

$$F = (\text{Capital} \times \text{Risk}\%) / \text{maximum drawdown}$$

Where the drawdown represents the amount of money that can be lost in trading, as a percentage of the available capital.

In the event that a trader with an available capital of 100,000 dollars decides to risk a maximum of 2% in each single operation, taking into account that their trading system has had a maximum statistical drawdown of 600 dollars, the calculation of the position sizing becomes:

F = (100,000 x 2%) / 600 = 3.33 contracts / shares

Chapter 15 - The History of Derivatives

A derivative instrument, in finance, indicates a financial security that derives its value from another financial asset or from an index (for example, stocks, financial indexes, currencies, interest rates or even commodities), called the underlying.

The main uses of derivative instruments are hedging against a financial risk, arbitrage (i.e. buying a product in one market and selling it in another market) and speculation.

The most popular derivative instruments are forwards, futures, options and swaps. Each of them is divided into subtypes. Derivatives are considered part of financial assets, i.e. assets of a financial nature; stocks, bonds and bank current accounts are also financial assets and today many of them are dematerialized and intangible.

The variables underlying the listing of derivative securities are called underlying assets and can be of different nature: they can be shares, bonds, financial indexes, commodities such as oil or even another derivative. There are derivatives based on the most diverse variables - even on the amount of snow that has fallen in a given area.

Derivatives are traded in many financial markets, and above all in markets outside the official stock exchange centers, that is, in alternative markets to actual stock exchanges, known as over the counter (OTC). There is therefore, in an abstract sense, a general derivatives market, alongside the securities / transferable securities market (shares and bonds) and composed of all markets for the various types of derivatives: futures, options and swaps (the same can be said for securities, of which there is a stock market and a bond market).

The derivative is a financial product

characterized by a high level of complexity, usually suitable for a competent investor, with a high propensity to risk and, above all, informed of the complicated contractual mechanisms underlying the functioning of the instrument.

The history of derivatives

Some forms of derivative instruments have ancient origins. In particular, forward contracts were also used in the times of the Greeks and Romans and the first organized markets for their exchange date back to the 17th and 18th centuries.The considerable diffusion that these instruments have known since the second half of the twentieth century is due to various factors.

- The end, in 1971, of the international fixed exchange rate system due to the fall of the Bretton Woods agreements, with the consequent emergence of the exchange rate risk, quite common in the context of international economic, financial and commercial transactions.

- The oil shocks of 1973 and 1979: the sudden sharp increases in the price of oil caused a parallel intensification of market risk, both due to the large fluctuations in prices and the consequent effects on inflation.

- The globalization of markets and the simultaneous introduction of computers, which allow you to quickly perform complex price calculations related to each other.

- The first notable diffusion of derivatives took place in the period 1989-1992, at the end of which their overall capitalization reached almost 20,000 billion dollars.

There was a slowdown after the huge losses suffered by large companies, such as Metallgesellschaft in 1993 and Procter & Gamble in 1994, and the bankruptcy of Barings Bank in 1995, but the expansion then resumed.

In December 2010 the volume of derivatives - more precisely, the total value of the assets underlying the derivatives - amounted to approximately 670,000 billion dollars, 601,048 of which for over the counter (OTC) derivatives, with a prevalence of interest rate swaps (364,378 billions of dollars). For a comparison, it can be considered that world GDP, around the year 2010, was estimated at around 70,000 billion dollars.

Chapter 16 - The Purpose of Derivatives

Derivatives can be used for three main purposes:

- risk coverage (hedging);
- speculation;
- arbitrage.

Let's look at them in greater detail.

Risk coverage

In general, it is said that those who buy take a long position, in the sense that by buying a commodity or a security, they expose themselves to the risk that the market price will decrease over time (I buy at 90, but the price gradually drops to 80); on the contrary, it is said that the seller takes a short position, in the sense that he exposes himself to the risk of a market rise (I sell today at 80, but if I had waited for tomorrow I could have sold at 85). Risk hedging takes place by taking a long position to balance the risk inherent in a transaction that involves taking a short position, and vice versa.

For example, company A enters into a contract that obliges it to purchase a certain quantity of coffee in three months at a fixed price (long position); the risk consists in the possibility that in three months the price of coffee will be lower than the one fixed now. To balance the risk, company A takes a parallel short position by committing to sell, to company B who in turn commits to buy that same quantity of coffee at a price slightly higher than that set in the first contract. In this way, company A forgoes the higher earnings that would derive from a sharp rise in the price of coffee, but protects itself from the risk of its decrease.

These commitments to sell and buy are derivative instruments in the sense that they have their own market, but any gains and losses arise from changes in the price of the so-called underlying (in the case of the example it is the price of coffee), not their own. The difference with a share is clear: if you buy a share, the decisive factor is the price of the share itself; if you buy a derivative, what decides is the price of the underlying.

Speculation

Derivatives can also be used for speculative purposes, taking advantage of what is called the leverage effect in finance. In general, the leverage effect is understood to mean the greater gain compared to the invested capital that is obtained if a transaction, which requires an investment of a certain amount, is carried out using debt for a large part of that amount. I.e. if the operation is carried out with the use of a limited amount of equity (the positive effect, however, occurs only if the operation is successful).

In the case of derivatives, the leverage effect consists in the fact that commitments or rights are assumed to buy or sell by paying amounts that amount to very small percentages (roughly from 2%

to 7%) of the value of the underlying asset.

Advantages

Referring to the example proposed above, subject A who undertakes to purchase the coffee could not carry out any operation of the opposite sign in order to protect themselves; They could in fact be convinced that the price of coffee will rise sharply in three months and "speculate" on the rise. They then enter into contracts that commit them to buy coffee for three months at a fixed price, paying a small percentage of the corresponding amount. If the price of coffee is really higher in three months, speculator A will make money. In fact, they will be able to buy coffee at a lower price than the market price and thus immediately resell it at a higher price.

Speculator A could buy a derivative on coffee. That is, they could commit to buying coffee in six months, for 5,000,000 dollars by paying an initial sum of 100,000. If in six months the price of coffee increases by 10%, the speculator will be able to buy coffee for 5,000,000 dollars and immediately sell it for 5,500,000 dollars, with a profit of 500,000 dollars. The leverage effect consists of this: if the derivative did not intervene and were bought today at 5,000,000 to resell in six months at 5,500,000, a gain of 10% would be realized, equivalent to 20% on an annual basis; if, on the other hand, a derivative is purchased, only 100,000 dollars are committed and the profit therefore amounts to 400% over six months, 800% on an annual basis.

Risks

However, a distinctly different scenario would arise if the price of coffee fell instead. Speculator A would have to make the purchase at a higher price than the market price. Not only would it be difficult for them to resell the coffee (in any case, having to sell it at a lower price, they would register a loss), but they could have made an excessive commitment: the amount to pay out to buy the coffee would in fact be much greater than he had already paid.

Note the difference with an investment in shares. If you buy shares for $100,000, the maximum loss you can suffer cannot exceed the amount paid. Instead, you can buy a derivative (that is, you can undertake the commitment to buy coffee, or other) for 5,000,000 dollars by paying only 100,000. However, if the price were to decrease by 10%, on the one hand you would have to pay 5,000,000 dollar to meet the commitment, on the other hand by reselling the underlying (coffee or other), you would only collect 4,500,000 dollars, with a loss of 500,000 dollars equal to five times the sum originally committed. Speculator B therefore risks finding themselves in a situation of insolvency, of going bankrupt.

In this regard, the case of the German MetallGesellschaft is known, which in 1993 carried out a similar speculation trusting in a prompt rise in the price of oil, which was falling, but the price instead continued to decline. The company only avoided bankruptcy thanks to a $1.9 billion bailout organized by 150 German and international banks.

Arbitrage

A third use is for arbitrage. In such cases, however, it is essentially a question of buying where the price is lower to immediately resell where the price is higher and the final effect is to equalize prices on the various markets.

Chapter 17 - Types of Derivatives

New derivatives arise every day, with different financial profiles and different degrees of sophistication. In jargon, the standard types are called plain vanilla, while the more complex types are called exotic. The best known and most popular types are:

- futures;
- forward rate agreement;
- swaps, especially Interest Rate Swaps and currency swaps;
- options.

Let's take a look at them one by one.

Futures

Futures contracts are similar to forward contracts. These are contracts that involve a commitment to buy or sell goods or financial assets on a certain date and at a predetermined price. Unlike a real forward contract, futures are standardized contracts regarding amounts and maturities and, moreover, refer to goods or financial assets indicated only in the characteristics (coffee of a certain type, not a specific batch of coffee; government bonds with a residual maturity of at least 15 years, not necessarily 15-year bonds issued today or 20-year bonds issued five years ago). They are distinguished into:

- financial futures, which have a financial underlying:
- interest rate futures for fixed income securities;
- currency futures for currencies;
- stock index futures for equity indexes;
- commodity futures, contracts that have foodstuffs (rice, coffee, cocoa, etc.), metals, oil, etc. as underlying.

Interest rate futures

Interest rate futures can be used to hedge risks arising from changes in interest rates, which can adversely affect the value of a portfolio of fixed income securities.

For example, a bank that purchases $1,000,000 newly issued government bonds is exposed to the risk of rising interest rates. The holders of the securities are in fact entitled to receive annual interest at a predetermined rate; in particular, if a twenty-year bond has a face value of $100 and offers 5% interest, its holder will collect $5 annually for twenty years. If the market interest rates do not vary, the holder can at any time sell the security at nominal value, as the new buyer will still earn 5% interest each year. However, if at a given moment the market interest rate on a security of the same duration increases to 7%, because the 5 dollars annual coupon together with the differential between the purchase price and the redemption price (equal to the nominal value) guarantee such a yield, the price of the securities purchased by the bank will have to fall according to the formula:

$$R = (C + (Vr - Pa) / n) / Pa \times 100$$

where:

- R = market yield (7%)
- C = coupon of the bond (5 %)
- Vr = reimbursement value of the security (100)
- n = residual duration of the security in years (e.g. 10).

Leaving aside the incidence of withholding taxes, it follows that the purchase price of the bond ten years after its maturity, in order to guarantee interest equal to market rates for ten-year bonds (7%), will have to drop to 88.23. An increase in interest rates therefore leads to a decrease in the market value of the securities, or a financial loss for the bank.

The bank can protect itself by selling ten futures contracts of $100,000 each (standard denomination), that is, in essence, by entering into a commitment to sell its securities for $1,000,000 on a set date. It is obviously necessary to find a buyer, therefore someone who is interested in defending themselves from the risk of a decrease in interest rates (or a speculator), but the conclusion of the operation is facilitated by the fact that there are ten distinct contracts, each of a standard denomination.

Furthermore, the transaction is not concluded directly with the counterparties, but with an intermediary structure such as a stock exchange (for the securities of the United States Government it is the Chicago Board of Trade).

The buyer and seller of a futures contract must make an initial security deposit, called the mandatory margin, of $2,000 for each contract (2%). Furthermore, the contracts are subjected to valuation every day according to market values (so-called marking to market); an increase in the price of the underlying entails a potential loss for those who committed to sell, a potential gain for those who committed to buy. The potential gain increases the escrow, the potential loss decreases it; if this decrease brings the deposit below the mandatory minimum value (equal to or slightly less than the initial deposit), the party facing the potential loss must pay enough money to restore the mandatory margin.

Currency futures

To understand the typical use of currency futures, one can think of an American company that has sold goods to a German company by agreeing on a payment of 1,000,000 euros after two months. After two months, the American company will receive euros that could be worth less as a result of changes in exchange rates and therefore, converted into dollars, entail a loss.

To protect itself from this risk, the American

company can enter into futures contracts that oblige it to sell (and at the same time oblige one or more counterparties to buy) 1,000,000 euros at two months at the current exchange rate. For example, it could enter into similar contracts with the Chicago Mercantile Exchange.

Stock index futures

Managers of mutual funds or pension funds and insurance companies make large and complex investments in shares and, therefore, are exposed to the risk of generalized falls in their prices, or falls in stock market indexes (so-called systematic risk).

Stock index futures contracts, which provide for the transfer of sums in cash, allow you to protect yourself. If person A sells a $250,000 contract on the S&P 500 Index on a maturity date, they agree to pay $250 for each point of what the index will be at maturity; the buyer accepts instead to pay $250 for each point of the current index. This implies that, if the index goes down, those who have sold earn (pay less than what they receive), if the index goes up, those who have bought gain.

Thus we see that the owner of a large and varied portfolio hedges themselves from the risk of a generalized fall in stock market prices by selling stock index futures. To understand the convenience to buy, we can think of a subject who, convinced of the rise of an index in three months, does not have liquidity to invest immediately; This person cannot therefore buy securities now, but can buy stock index futures as, to do so, it must pay only the mandatory margin (similarly to what happens for interest rate futures and, in general, for futures contracts). If the stock market index actually goes up, this will allow them to make a gain similar to what they would have made if he could have bought stocks now and resold them after three months.

Commodity futures

These are derivatives whose underlying assets are traded globally, such as oil or coffee. Their mechanics have already been illustrated in the section on the purpose of derivatives. Other aspects, such as the margin mechanism, are similar to those in use for other futures contracts.

Forward Rate Agreement

The forward rate agreement, also briefly called FRA, is a contract by which two parties undertake to exchange an amount in money which is determined on the basis of the difference between an agreed fixed rate (contract rate) and a reference rate such as LIBOR.

Whoever buys an FRA undertakes to pay an amount commensurate with the agreed rate, whoever sells it undertakes to pay an amount commensurate with the reference rate. Upon expiry, settlement takes place by difference: if the buyer has to pay 1000 and the seller 1100, the seller will pay the difference of 100 to the buyer.

The buyer could be a person who has

contracted a debt regulated at a variable rate; if this rate rises, the buyer of the FRA receives from the counterparty an amount similar to the higher interest that he must pay to his creditor. The seller could be a person who has granted loans at a variable rate; if this rate falls, it receives from the buyer an amount similar to the lower interest it receives from its debtor.

Swap

In general, swap contracts commit the contracting parties to exchange future monetary flows. The two main types are interest rate swaps and currency swaps.

Interest rate swap

In an interest rate swap, the two parties agree to exchange periodic cash flows calculated as interest on a notional reference capital. In particular, one party undertakes to pay interest calculated on this capital at a fixed rate, the other undertakes to pay interest calculated at a variable rate.

To understand the convenience of contracting such transactions, we can think of two financial intermediaries:

- Bank A gets into short-term debt (for example on the interbank market) and makes long-term loans (for example mortgages); it would therefore be in difficulty in the event of a rise in short-term rates;

- Financial company B borrows in the long term (e.g. by issuing bonds) and lends in the short term (e.g. by financing the purchase of consumer goods); it would therefore find itself in difficulty in the event of a decrease in short-term rates.

The contract that can benefit both of them has the following characteristics:

- Bank A undertakes to pay to finance company B, for ten years, periodic amounts calculated as interest at a fixed rate; this allows the financial company to obtain flows that still allow it to honor its long-term debt;

- Finance company B undertakes to pay to bank A, for ten years, periodic amounts calculated as interest at a rate equal to LIBOR plus half a point; this allows the bank to obtain flows that allow it to bear the burden of short-term loans.

The contract just described is called a coupon swap. There are also different schemes such as the basis swap, in which the two contracting parties recognize amounts calculated on two different variable rates, the zero coupon swap, in which the flows calculated at the fixed rate are paid in a single solution at maturity, etc.

Interest rate swaps are by far the most popular derivatives. As of December 2010, their total value ($364.378 billion) was more than half the total volume of derivatives.

Currency swap

They are similar to interest rate swaps but, in addition to having as their object the exchange of flows in different currencies, they provide for flows of capital as well as interest: there is an initial exchange of capital in different currencies, then a period of flows of interest, finally the return of the originally exchanged capital.

Options

Options, unlike futures, give their purchaser the right, not the obligation, to buy or sell the underlying on a certain date (called European options) or by a certain date (called American), at a fixed price. Call options confer the right to buy, put options the right to sell. The main features are:

- the underlying asset, which can be of the most varied types: commodities, currencies, government bonds, stock market indexes, interest rates, etc., but more often futures;

- the strike price;
- the expiration date;
- the premium, which represents the purchase price of the contract and is typically paid at the time of signing.

In the case of an European call option, the buyer can choose at maturity whether:

- exercise the option right by purchasing the underlying at the strike price, if this is lower than the market price;
- renounce the purchase, as well as the premium paid.

Similarly, in the case of a put option, the buyer can choose at maturity whether to:

- exercise the option right, selling the underlying at the strike price, if this is higher than the market price;

- renounce the sale, as well as the premium paid.

In the case of American options, you can exercise the right to buy or sell even before the expiration, you can let the expiration run if you are not interested. In any case, the buyer of an option risks the premium at the most while it can theoretically face significant gains.

The seller's position is quite different and substantially opposite. They certainly gets the prize, but:

- If they sell a call option, they absolutely undertakes to sell the underlying at the strike price, and this will happen just when it is lower than the market price (they will have to sell "below cost");

- If they sell a put option, they absolutely

undertake to buy the underlying at the strike price, and this will happen just when it is higher than the market price.

The seller of options, be they call or put, therefore risks theoretically unlimited losses.

Chapter 18 - Derivatives Market

The first market to trade derivatives was the CBOT founded in 1848. They are traded both on the stock exchange and in over-the-counter markets and are generally characterized by financial leverage, thus representing financial instruments of particular risk. Furthermore, the markets on which they are traded are normally characterized by much less liquidity than the stock market, and even worse for typically "tailored" derivatives (for example swaps, which are "tailor-made"). They are often conceptually equated to bets, rather than to "investments".

The mass of derivatives circulating in the world would amount to between 600,000 and 700,000 billion dollars in 2013, even if the real quantification is uncertain, due to the very nature of these securities.

This number refers to the notional or nominal value of derivatives, the theoretical maximum value, while the gross market position of global derivatives amounts to one fifth of global GDP: it represents how much it would cost to detect, at market prices, all existing contracts. The net position is worth 10% of the gross position.

The difference is clear when considering a lottery ticket: the face value is the amount of the first prize, which does not take into account the probability-risk of the event that can be cashed, while the gross position is the selling price of the ticket.

Alan Greenspan initiated the issuance and dissemination of derivatives. The particularity of a security on existing mortgages and mortgages is detectable, and of nominal assets recorded in balance sheet assets even if they do not represent real entities, unlike shares and bonds which are at least theoretically linked to investments in real assets.

A potential problem with derivatives is that they include an ever-increasing notional amount of assets, which can influence and lead to distortions in the underlying capital and equities of the markets themselves. Investors begin to look at derivative markets to decide whether to buy or sell stocks, and so what was originally a market to transfer risk now becomes a leading indicator.

US legislation provides for the denomination of a pension fund for private financial institutions that invest at least 25% of their capital in financial entities that are themselves classified as pension funds, which are subject to prudential limitations in their investment choices in defense of capital. Due to the high risk, a derivative should be present in pension fund investments only to protect against a higher opposite risk: more directly the fund if it really followed a prudent and low-risk investment policy, it would not need derivatives to protect itself (it would avoid the high risk and that's it). In particular, the sale of derivatives to non-qualified parties is questionable, given the difficulty of correctly determining the correct market value, particularly difficult in the case of exotic derivatives. and structured.

Some pension funds claim to invest in derivatives for the purpose of increasing revenue in the face of market fluctuations. A study by the Bank of New York and Casey, Quirk & Associates predicts an increase in investment by private companies in derivatives from $ 5 billion to $300 billion for the year 2022. Individuals and companies, almost always lacking sophisticated financial knowledge, normally have no way of correctly determining the pricing of exotic and structured derivatives, nor of assessing their risk.

Chapter 19 - The Basics of Options

In finance with the term option, we mean that particular type of contract that gives the holder the right, but not the obligation (therefore precisely the "option"), to buy or sell the security on which the option it is recorded, called the underlying instrument (or simply the underlying), at a certain predetermined price (strike price or simply strike) by a certain date, against a non-recoverable premium paid. Options can have the most diverse underlyings: shares, commodities, interest rates, etc.

The fundamental difference of options with respect to other derivative instruments consists in the right of withdrawal of the holder. In fact, they are not obliged to buy (or sell) the underlying, but they can do so if exercising the option derives an effective economic advantage. For this reason they are also called asymmetric derivative securities.

Type of options

Options confer the right to buy (call type) or sell (put type) a security (or underlying) at a predetermined price (or strike) within a defined date. By buying call options or selling put options you can take bullish positions; conversely, one can take bearish positions by selling calls or buying puts.

An option is to all intents and purposes a contract that is stipulated between two market players. In fact, this contract is characterized by the underlying instrument, the duration of the contract, the strike price of the option and the premium paid for this contract.

The right to exercise the option may either be limited only to expiration ("European option"), or extended to all the time elapsing until expiration ("American option").

Advantages

Options are widely used for speculative purposes or as financial hedges in medium / high risk investments: for example, an importer can hedge / protect themselves (at least partially) from the exchange rate risk in the long term by signing an option on the price of the commodity subject import if the purchase of the same is distant in time; this allows the importer not to purchase either the asset or the currency in advance and even not to purchase it at all in the event of economic inconvenience upon expiry of the option, thus losing only the initial cost on the option contract itself and thus limiting any major losses.

In the event of the purchase of call options, in fact, the maximum possible loss is the premium paid plus the trading commissions due to the intermediary, while the gain is theoretically unlimited. On the contrary, in the case of the sale of call options, the maximum gain is the premium paid by the buyer while the possible loss is unlimited. In the case of the purchase of put options, which give the right to sell the underlying asset at the strike price, there is a maximum gain of the same price minus the cost of the contract. In the case of the sale of put options there is the initial income of the cost of stipulating the contract, upon expiration there is a zero income if the strike price is lower than the value of the underlying asset.

Evaluation of the option

Obviously, the convenience or otherwise of exercising the option by the buyer / seller at the end or within the time limits will essentially depend on the difference between the exercise price of the option or the strike price, initially stipulated in the option contract, and the final effective value of the underlying asset at maturity. Crucial then becomes the more or less correct valuation of the price of an option based on the current value of the underlying asset and the estimated future value. In particular, the treatment of the option price is the subject of a vast mathematical literature in which the Cox-Ross-Rubistein models (also called binomial model) and the Black and Scholes formula are particularly well established, despite some intrinsic limitations. There are also new models, the results of which correspond to those of the Black and Scholes formula and the binomial model, but which are much easier to use from the user's point of view, these are, for example, the Datar-Mathews method (2007) and the fuzzy return method for the valuation of real options (2008).

There are numerous variations of the basic option definition, also called the plain vanilla option, and they are represented by exotic options.

The contractual aspect

The option is a stock exchange contract under which the writer or seller assigns to the buyer or proposer the right to sell (put option) or buy (call option) a certain amount of financial or real assets, underlying assets, at a predetermined base price or exercise price, (strike price or exercise price), commodities and forward contracts (futures).

The underlying asset must have a market with official and publicly recognized prices; typically, options are built on stocks, currencies, interest rates, commodities, and futures.

The buyer, by purchasing a call option, acquires the right to purchase the asset underlying the contract; vice versa, by buying a put option (place) acquires the right to sell it. The subscriber, on the other hand, at the request of the buyer, must sell them the asset underlying the contract that has signed a call option, vice versa they must buy it if they have subscribed a put option. The buyer acquires a right which they can exercise (if convenient), or abandon if not, losing only the premium. The seller of an option can register a maximum profit equal to the premium received, while theoretically he can lose indefinitely. To calculate the profit possibly deriving from the exercise of an option, it is necessary to consider the disbursement constituted by the premium, which is greater the further the contract expires and the higher the market price is a call) or lower (in the case of a put) than the base price.

The value of an option and the sensitivity coefficients

The value of an option is a function of six factors:

- The strike price
- The market price on the underlying asset of the option contract itself
- The time remaining until the option expires
- The volatility of the price of the underlying asset
- The risk-free short-term rate of return
- Dividends expected during the life of the option

The Greeks

The sensitivity coefficients of the options, also known as Greeks, summarize the variation in the value of the option when one of the factors varies by one unit, also known as the sensitivity of the value of an option. More on this in the next chapters.

The convenience of exercising the option

Depending on the relationship between the strike price and the market price, the options are defined:

- In the money when the holder would have the convenience to exercise the option if it were at maturity
- At the money when the holder is in a position of indifference
- Out of the money when the holder would not have the convenience to exercise the option if it were at maturity.

The convenience is given by the difference between the exercise price (Pe) and the market price (Pm) and is the opposite in the case of a put or call.

Basically, we have:

- Pe = Pm At the money - At the money
- Pe <Pm In the money - Out of the money
- Pe> Pm Out of the money - In the money

Chapter 20 - Exotic options

The simple European and American options (called "plain vanilla") are rarely used. More often, complex structure options are used, called exotic.

The "exoticism" of this type of options is represented by additional clauses that can

- evaluate the evolution of the share price (path-dependent options)
- define some limits of validity.

The growing complexity of the financial markets has led to a proliferation of this type of instrument. Rubinstein (1992) suggests the identification of 11 possible categories, but in light of the fast dynamics with which the segment develops, this classification can only be partial. There are options packages, binary options, path dependent options, compound options, options on more than one underlying asset and many more.

An example of an exotic path-dependent option is the Asian option, where the payoff depends on the average price of the underlying over the period considered. Various approaches can be followed to evaluate exotic options. For some classes of exotic options it is possible to write a valuation formula in a closed form, which can be obtained assuming that you are operating in a market that in literature is called the Black-Scholes environment. For other categories of exotic options, even supposing to operate in the Black - Scholes environment it is not possible to calculate the expected profit. In such cases, numerical methods must be used for evaluation, such as Monte Carlo and quasi-Monte Carlo simulation techniques, the construction of binary decision trees or the discretization of the differential equations that regulate the price of options.

Below is a succinct list of exotic options, with their definition, without claiming to be exhaustive as this market is characterized by the very frequent creation of new instruments.

Asian options

With the Asian options we intend to evaluate the evolution of the asset in terms of average. This evaluation can be made at the strike level, equating the latter to the average: in this case we speak of average strike options. Alternatively, this valuation can be made at the term level with which the strike is compared: in fact, if the strike price is normally compared with the current price of the underlying, it is possible to replace the latter with the average price; this is the case with average rate options.

Associated with the Asian options there are a series of additional clauses that determine some instrumental aspects, such as the type of average, whether the average is weighted or not, whether the detection is continuous or discrete.

Barrier options

Barrier clauses can be added to any type of

option. Associated with a price limit (i.e. when the underlying crosses a certain price up or down), the start or end of validity is determined. With a barrier of type in we mean to determine the moment in which the option begins to be valid: for example a down-and-in option indicates an option that begins to be valid when the price of the underlying falls below a certain value. Vice versa an option of type out.

As in the previous case, additional clauses determine the type of detection that is made on the value of the underlying (continuous or discrete detection).

Compound options

A compound option is an option written on another derivative security. All combinations are possible: put on put, put on call and so on. A particular type is the chooser option, in which the underwriter can determine whether to buy / sell a call or a put. A compound option can of course have all the other characteristics of the other options (European / American, barrier, Asian etc.)

Binary Options

A binary option has the characteristic of not evaluating the gain in differential terms (for example in the case of the call the gain can be understood as the difference between the market value and the strike) but the revenue is fixed when a certain threshold value (a fixed amount of money is collected as long as the underlying exceeds a certain value).

These options are also called digital options.

Lookback options

In lookback options, the value of the strike price is equal to the maximum or minimum (obviously depending on the type of option) of the prices assumed by the underlying asset during the period of validity of the option itself. Variants of this kind of options are partial lookbacks for which the maximum or minimum is multiplied by a factor less than 1, thus dampening the possible gain.

Bermuda options

In Bermuda options, exercise is only allowed on certain dates or during specific time intervals; they fall into the category of American non-standard options.

Average-rate options

These are Vanilla options for which the arithmetic average of the prices measured is used instead of the price at maturity of the underlying.

Chapter 21 - The Greeks

In a previous chapter we have mentioned the Greeks. In this chapter, we dive deeper into them.

Delta

The first indicator to look out for is the delta of an option. The delta, expressed as a percentage of the price of the underlying, shows how much a contract appreciates in absolute value in conjunction with a small appreciation of the underlying market. It is therefore an indicator of the option's sensitivity to price movements of the asset on which it is written.

To give an example of the Ftse Mib index as a "cash" market, the premium of an option with a delta equal to 50% would appreciate by 100 points if the index grew by 200 points.

This is for calls; it goes without saying that for

put options the delta is negative. In fact they depreciate when the underlying market appreciates. The delta goes hand in hand with the status (moneyness) of the option: an atm ("at the money") option has a delta that is around 50%; an itm ("in the money") contract is instead characterized by a delta between 50 and 100%, the closer to 100 the more itm is; conversely, an otm ("out of the money") option has a delta between zero and 50%, the closer to zero the more otm it is.

Gamma

Complementary to the delta, the gamma measures how much the delta varies as the underlying market changes. This is because the delta of an option is not a fixed value, but changes mainly according to the movements of the underlying; in fact, by varying the prices of the underlying, the status (moneyness) of a contract also changes. In fact, an atm option can thus become otm, or itm, thus causing a change in its sensitivity towards the movements of the underlying. To stay in the previous example, if the same contract on the Ftse Mib index had had a range of 1.5%, the new delta of the option would have been equal to 51.5%. The delta therefore increased due to the appreciation of the underlying market, which made itm what was previously an atm option.

Vega

Volatility is also a very important element in the pricing of an option; the vega measures how much the premium of a contract would appreciate as the volatility of the underlying market increases by 1%. The vega can be calculated in absolute form, thus expressing the appreciation of the premium in points; or as a percentage, thus indicating the percentage appreciation of the premium.

The expression in percentage form is preferable when constructing the strategy because it allows to compare directly, and in a homogeneous way, the characteristics of the various contracts on which the negotiation can fall, while the absolute form is more suitable for close trading on a single option.

To give an example, a contract with a premium of 1,000 points and vega of 5% would appreciate by 5%, call or put, if the volatility of the underlying market increases by one percentage point. It is obvious that the vega can be both positive (which indicates a bullish position on volatility, as is the case with the purchase of an option), and negative (which indicates a bearish position on volatility, as happens in the case of a sale to the overdraft of a contract).

Theta

As we know, the passage of time causes a natural depreciation of the option; the theta measures precisely what is the loss in value of the contract from one day to the next. Like vega, theta can also be expressed in absolute form (and therefore in terms of the value of the premium), or as a percentage of the option premium itself. Here too the same considerations made regarding the vega apply. Therefore we expect, for example, that a contract with a theta of -0.5%, call or put, will lose value by 0.5% the next day. It is quite intuitive that theta is negative, thus playing against the investor, in case of purchase of options; vice versa it is positive, playing in favor of the investor, in the event that options are sold short.

Leverage

The last operating indicator is intended to measure the degree of amplification of the results offered by the contract compared to what would be obtained with a similar investment on the underlying market; it therefore expresses the degree of the classic leverage effect, typical of derivative instruments. Calculated as the ratio between the price of the underlying and the premium of the option, then multiplied by the delta of the contract, it shows by how much the percentage change in the underlying must be multiplied to obtain the corresponding return on the derivative. Against a net leverage of 20 times and an appreciation of 5% of the underlying market, for example, the call contract in question would realize a return of 100% compared to the capital initially invested. Conversely, it would be a loss if we were talking about put options.

Chapter 22 - Intrinsic and Extrinsic Value

The value of a financial option is determined by three main factors: intrinsic value, time and volatility. By value we mean the amount that is paid or collected for the purchase or sale of an option. It is essentially the premium.

Let's start with the definition of intrinsic value and extrinsic value.

The determination of the intrinsic value depends on the strike of the option (the exercise price) and the price of the underlying security. For calls, it derives from the subtraction between the price of the security and the strike of the option, therefore:

Asset Price - Option Strike = Intrinsic Value

Let's take an example.

We are interested in the ABC stock which currently is worth 64 USD, and we decide to buy a CALL with ITM strike at 60 USD, for which we pay 6 USD. We then determine the intrinsic value of the option we have just purchased:

64 USD (the price of the stock) - 60 USD (strike of the option) = 4 USD

4 USD corresponds to the intrinsic value of the call we purchased. If the stock's price goes up, its intrinsic value will also increase as a result.

Depending on whether it is a call option or a put option, the calculation of the intrinsic value is different. As we have just seen, for calls the strike must be subtracted from the price of the stock, while for puts the opposite is true, that is, the price of the stock must be subtracted from the strike.

Intrinsic Value Call: Stock Price - Call Strike

Intrinsic value Put: Strike of the Put- Price of the stock

The calculation can only be applied to ITM options, since ATMs and OTMs have no intrinsic value but only temporal value, which decreases as the expiration approaches until it reaches zero. Only ITM options when they expire do not go to zero. If the intrinsic value of an ITM option is very very high, it is defined as Deep In The Money.

Intrinsic value helps determine whether it is better to sell an option or hold it until it expires. As we will see in the next chapter, the time factor plays a very important role.

The extrinsic value is also defined as a time value. The defining factors are the intrinsic value of the option and the option premium. It is calculated by subtracting the intrinsic value from the premium paid, therefore:

Premium paid - Intrinsic value = Time value

Going back to the example above, if we subtracted the 4 USD obtained from the intrinsic value calculation from the 6 USD paid to buy the call option, we would obtain 2 USD, which corresponds to the time value.

This is therefore the value to be paid in order to reserve the right to act for one's own advantage on the underlying asset within a certain period of time, regardless of market conditions.

Chapter 23 - Time Decay

As we have already mentioned, intrinsic value, time and volatility play a key role. After analyzing the intrinsic and extrinsic values we then see the time decay, the implied volatility and the historical volatility.

As we know, options lose value as they approach their expiration date. This process is called time decay.

This has different consequences depending on whether it is ITM, ATM or OTM options. ITM options close to expiration see the time value drop to 0, thus remaining only with intrinsic value. In ATM options, and also in OTM options, on the other hand, since the intrinsic value is equal to 0, these lose their value completely with the approach of expiry.

There are two types of volatility, implied and

historical.

Historical volatility refers to the price movements of the underlying in relation to a given period of time. Usually the historical volatility values are indicated as a percentage, and indicate the change in the price of the security with respect to a given period.

For example, if we were monitoring the performance of the ABC stock, which is currently quoted at $100, with a one-month historical volatility value of 40%, this would mean that the price could probably go from $100 to $60 or from $100 to $140 in one month.

Implied volatility indicates the price movements of the underlying expected from the market based on available data. For example, before the announcement of the earnings it usually increases, because there is uncertainty about the data but then, once made public, it usually decreases. The definition of implied volatility is linked to the value of the options, as it helps to define their price.

It is mainly determined by the expectations of market movements also in relation to a certain period of time, so it indicates the percentage of variation that is expected, and in this way it affects the price of the option that you are going to buy.

Depending on the expiration of the option, there will be a different implied volatility, due to the different expectations in relation to the time defined by the expiry.

Summarizing what has been seen in this chapter and in the previous one, the value of an option, understood as the premium that is paid / received from the purchase / sale, is determined by various factors: intrinsic and extrinsic values, time decay, implicit and historical volatility. These factors can be monitored and controlled and allow us to choose the option we want to operate with.

Chapter 24 - Volatility

There is no doubt that trading on volatility in recent years has brought considerable economic returns to those who adopted this strategy. It is no coincidence that professional traders (especially American ones), merchant bank trading rooms and hedge funds use volatility tools to their fullest. So let's try to make a very brief summary of these tools, necessarily sacrificing a little rigor on the altar of simplification and disclosure. By "brief" we do not mean the classic volatility indicators that traders use to evaluate price movements (eg the Average True Range. or the Bollinger Bands), but rather the implied volatility of the options or the historical volatility. But let's go in order.

The options have a so-called "implicit volatility" (often indicated with the Greek letter "sigma", σ) which in very simplified terms (the purists of the subject will forgive me) represents the future expectation of the price movements of the underlying asset. If traders expect greater price variability in the future (therefore greater volatility), the premium that the option buyer has to pay increases in order to have the opportunity to buy or sell the underlying in the future at a pre-established price today. In other words, the premium to be paid to purchase the option (call or put) increases. The pricing of the options also depends on other factors (e.g. price of the underlying, strike price, time to expiration, etc.), but the implied volatility (which, as mentioned, reflects the expectations of price variability) is of fundamental importance in determining the price. For our purposes for the moment we just need to know this.

I invite the curious reader to deepen the subject elsewhere. In addition to implied volatility, there is also "historical volatility" which is defined as the X-day standard deviation of returns. If historical volatility is calculated on daily data, to obtain an "annualized" value, the standard deviation is multiplied by the square root of 252 (number of average days of market opening). Historical volatility is an indicator of the past riskiness of the markets and is used as the denominator in the calculation of the Sharpe Ratio (unfortunately little known to traders, but widely used by investors). Historical and implied volatility are "conceptually different" as the first represents the change in past returns, while the second represents (simplifying) the expectation of changes in the prices themselves.

Let's see an important application of implied volatility. The world's leading stock index is the S&P 500 (ticker Bloomberg SPX, Yahoo ^ GSPC), which summarizes the performance of the 500 major American stocks listed on the NYSE, Amex and Nasdaq. These shares also have options listed on the Chicago Board Options Exchange (CBOE). The index itself also has options listed on the CBOE. The weighted average of the implied volatility of the short-term SPX options is grouped into an index, calculated by the CBOE, which is called the CBOE

Volatility Index better known as "VIX Index" . The VIX is also called the "fear index". On Yahoo Finance you can find the quotation with the ticker VIX. The methods of calculation of the VIX Index have changed over time, but the history is still available since 1990 (even if there are unofficial reconstructions even earlier).

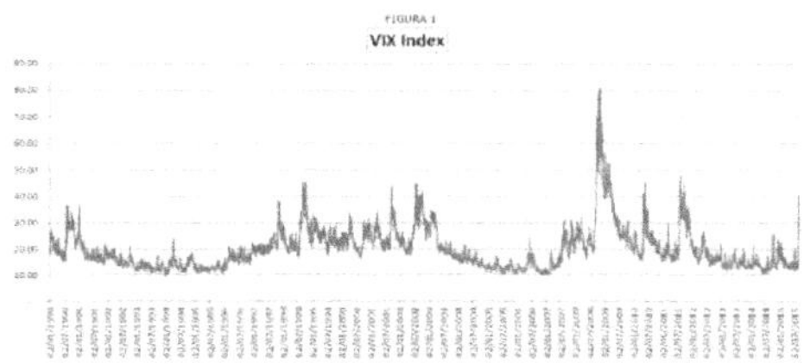

In picture 1 the historical graph of the VIX Index (data source Yahoo Finance, or CBOE.com). Despite the conceptual difference described above, the trend of implied volatility (represents for the S&P 500 from the VIX Index) and that of historical volatility, with the same time interval (30 days), tend to be strongly correlated.

It should be noted that historical volatility is

easily calculated by anyone on any underlying with a simple Excel sheet and is available in many trading platforms, while the implied volatility is a little more complicated for mere mortals to derive. It should also be noted that there is also some correlation between historical volatility and the Average True Range indicator, although this correlation is less evident.

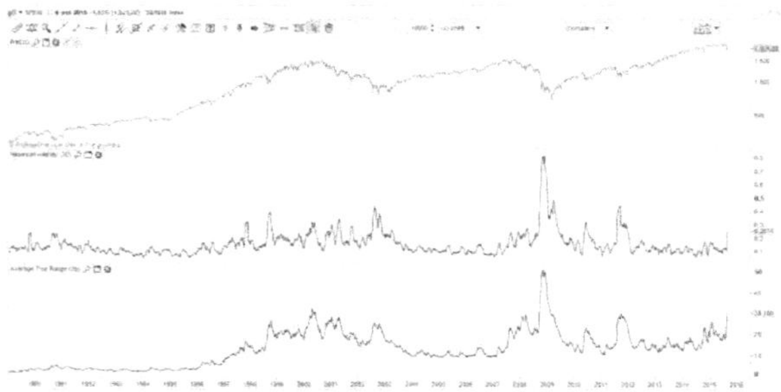

The reason for this difference lies in the fact that in a hypothetical market that were to rise very rapidly, with large green candles of comparable height, the ATR would assume high values, while the historical volatility would be almost zero, lacking the assumption of the variability of returns.

Simplifying, we can say that the VIX measures fear, because it measures the future expectation of the volatility of the S&P 500 index and consequently of the shares that make it up. In principle, volatility means "alternation of price movements" which could be either upward or downward. However history teaches us that the increase of volatility corresponds to the decrease in prices, this is in line with the common thought that associates a greater danger to bearish markets.

Chapter 25 - Monte Carlo Methods

Hearing the word Monte Carlo on television, one immediately thinks of the famous district of the Principality of Monaco, a symbol of the jet set, wealth and fashion, which has become famous all over the world thanks to the Formula 1 Grand Prix. Not everyone knows, however , that this geographical place - and in particular the casino of the same name - gave the name to a wide class of computational methods for solving mathematical algorithms, invented in the 1940s and used in the most disparate fields of knowledge. More specifically, the so-called Monte Carlo methods were invented by physicists who worked in the Los Alamos laboratories during the Second World War, including the Nobel laureate Enrico Fermi, who was one of the first to use them to study the scattering of neutrons at the inside the graphite, but without leaving any publications to posterity.

The features of the Monte Carlo methods

Therefore, born from physics, they later spread to many branches of knowledge, from inferential statistics to stochastic optimization, from molecular chemistry to complex systems, i.e. those systems whose evolution cannot be described except by considering the interaction between the variables. at stake, due to the large number of agents. More specifically, Monte Carlo simulations are used when the paths of both continuous and discrete time dynamic stochastic systems are studied. Monte Carlo-type processes are simulated with any high-level programming language, such as C ++, Python, MATLAB, Julia, or others.

The simulation can be divided into four distinct steps:

- Generation of pseudo-random numbers (the pseudo prefix indicates that in their origin process there is in any case a deterministic succession at the base);
- Transformation into random variables;

- Generation of specific paths based on the domain;
- Output analysis.

Only the first step is common to all Monte Carlo methods, while the subsequent ones differ according to the system taken into consideration.

The most common methods for generating pseudo-random numbers are three: Van Der Corput, Halton and Sobol. These produce "low discrepancy" sequences, i.e. such that the proportion of the numbers generated in an interval of any size is proportional to the size of the interval itself. In a simpler way, an indispensable condition of these distributions is their homogeneity: there must not be regions of space in which there is a concentration of numbers higher than the others, as happens for example in the case of a normal distribution. Subsequently, the outputs are transformed into normal standards or into other probability distributions (Poisson, polylogarithmic, exponential), according to the system considered.

Without going into the details of the high-level mathematical formalism, the idea at stake is that by solving the equations we have analytical representations of the possible evolutions of the time of a physical system: these results are compared with the homologues obtained by the Monte Carlo methods, in the which is generally estimated the probability distribution from previously known data. The more coherent the two results are, the more accurate the simulation can be considered, always starting from the assumption that, especially in random systems such as the stock one, there is obviously nothing certain.

Applications in finance

A very interesting example is represented by a vanilla put or call option, whose stock price can be modeled through stochastic differential equations, such as the Black-Scholes model. Having therefore mathematical knowledge of the sample, payoff predictions can be made. This is useful for example in the case of Asian options, where you do not have analytical knowledge but can only perform the Monte Carlo simulation.

In the particular case, a statistical method called "control variables" is used, in which we want to know the expectation value of a random variable having known the average value of another random variable correlated with the first. To calculate the payoff of this derivative security, two different averages can be used, the arithmetic and the geometric one, obtaining a very complex formula for the price trend over time.

Chapter 26 - What Influences the Price of an Option

When purchasing an option, a premium is required in favor of the seller. The premium, which represents the option price, can be split into two components: the intrinsic value and the time value. Specifying the composition of the value of an option will allow you to better understand which factors are decisive and on which components they act.

Intrinsic Value and Temporal Value

Considering an option contract, the intrinsic value is defined as the value of the option in the event of immediate exercise. An in the money option has a positive intrinsic value while an out of the money option has a null intrinsic value. For example, a call option with an exercise price of $10 written on an underlying with a current value of $11, will have an intrinsic value of $1. Changes in the current price of the option or the strike price affect its amount.

The Time Value of an option is calculated as the difference between the option price and its intrinsic value. In fact, the value of an out of the money option can be identified precisely with its time value as its intrinsic value is null. The factors that influence the time value are the change in interest rates, the duration of life at maturity, the dividends distributed and the volatility of the underlying.

The intrinsic value of an option is mainly influenced by two variables:

- The current price of the underlying, S;
- The strike price, K;

Taking the previous example, by signing a Call with a Strike price of $10 and expiring in a future time T. As before, the current value of the underlying is $11 and therefore, an intrinsic value of $11 - $10 = $1 (S - K). Now, the price of the underlying varies from $11 to $12. We can easily derive that the new intrinsic value of the option will be $2 and will therefore be increased.

Now suppose, instead, to subscribe to a new Call option, always on the same underlying with a value of $11, but a Strike price of $13. In this case the intrinsic value will be $11 - $13 = $-2 (S - K) and therefore null.

It can be summarized by saying that for a call option, all other conditions being equal:

an increase in the price of the underlying (S) leads to an increase in the value of the option;

an increase in the strike price (K) leads to a decrease in the value of the option.

For a put option, the opposite is true.

The factors that influence the time value of an option

The time value of an option is mainly influenced by 4 factors:

- The residual life, T;

- The volatility of the price of the underlying, σ;
- The risk-free interest rate, r;
- The dividends expected during the life of the option, whose current value is D.

The residual life of the option affects American and European type contracts differently. In fact, if for an American option (both call and put) when T moves away, the value of the option is seen to increase, for an European this is not always the case.

A longer life span allows the owner to take advantage of more exercise opportunities than those with a shorter term. Therefore, he will have a better chance that his contract is in the money at the time of exercise. The possibility of exercising one's right, for the European typology, only at the predetermined date, however, makes the longer life at maturity an element that is not always favorable. In fact, with the passing of T, unfavorable situations could arise for the investor such as, in the case of a call, the distribution of dividends. It is therefore not possible to know whether a longer life is favorable or not for an European option.

Let us now consider the volatility of the underlying price. It can be defined as the measure of uncertainty regarding the future price behavior of a security and, therefore, of the extent of its fluctuations. For example, observe for the month of January the volatility of two securities which have the same initial and final value.

An increase in volatility leads to an increase in the probability that the stock's performance is very modest or very bright. Instead, for the holder of the underlying, these effects tend to offset each other, but not for the holder of an option. For the latter, the maximum loss is identifiable with the premium paid to the seller. The buyer of a Call will have a limited downside risk, while it will be able to make substantial gains in the event of significant increases in the price of the underlying. Mirror reasoning is done for the holder of a Put. So much so that the person most at risk is certainly the one who sells the option, who will ask for a higher price for their subscription. Therefore, the price of Calls and Puts will always be higher as volatility increases.

The risk-free interest rate compared to the other variables acts less clearly. It is fair to assume that an increase in the free risk rate leads to an increase in the price of the Calls and a decrease in the price of the Put. However, it should be remembered that all of this is considered valid on equal terms. Therefore, the effect that a change in the risk free rate has on share prices is not considered. The fluctuations in the interest rate are in fact one of the causes that lead to changes in the prices of the securities underlying the options. In particular, an increase in the free risk rate generally involves a decrease in share prices, conversely a decrease increases their value. Therefore, analyzing the net effect that derives from the two observations, we can have a particular case: an increase in the risk-free rate leads to a decrease in the price of the share, which induces a reduction in the price of a call option and vice versa.

The last factor of influence are dividends. The relationship between the expected dividends and the price of the Call or Put concerns the effect that their detachment has on the price of the underlying (in this case shares). On the predetermined day for the distribution of dividends, the share price will suffer a decrease in its value and therefore this will be harmful for a Call option and favorable for a Put option. The link that therefore binds the expected dividends and the price of a call is negative, while it is positive if placed in relation to a Put.

Chapter 27 - An Important Date in the Options World

Triple witching day (also called Triple Witching Friday or Day of the Three Witches) occurs on the third Friday in the last month of each quarter (March, June, September and December). It corresponds to the simultaneous expiration (or rollover) of various futures and options contracts.

Many US stock index futures, stock index options, and stock options expire on these exact days. The simultaneous expiration of the three different markets is the reason why these days are called "triple witching". However, with the addition of single stock futures contracts in 2002, which also expire on the third Friday every three months, the triple witching day is sometimes referred to as quadruple witching.

"The day of the four witches" is the most

accurate term, but the term has never caught on in the industry. Therefore, Triple Witching Day remains the most commonly used term among traders.

The event causes strong volatility on US markets, with possible strong repercussions also on world markets.

What is the day of the three witches?

The day of the three witches occurs four times a year, every third Friday in March, June, September and December. Due to its implications, triple witching day is also known as 'freaky Friday' among investors.

As anticipated, three types of instruments expire every third Friday of the months in question:

- index futures;
- stock index options;
- share options.

Hence the nickname of the day of the "three

witches".

The hour of the three witches is identified in the last hour of the US session (3:00-4:00 New York time).

The effects of the Triple Witching Day

Contracts for futures and options, unlike stocks, have an expiration date. During the term of these contracts, traders place their bets and triple witching day is the day when they have to decide whether to renew their futures contracts (holding a position in an unexpired contract) or close the position (which could buy or sell, depending on the direction of your original positioning).

Options traders, on the same days, also find out whether their position will close at a gain or a loss. On the day of the three witches, traders with high positions on such contracts may be financially incentivized to try to temporarily push the underlying market in a certain direction in order to influence the value of their contracts.

Given the unusual situation due to the simultaneous expiration of these contracts, the day of the three witches is carefully observed by investors, especially due to the unusual increase in trading which leads to a sharp peak in volatility.

It is advisable not to try to predict price movements during triple witching, as market conditions do not suggest any correct indications.

The growth in trading volumes, in fact, is due more to market speculation than to a change in the valuation of the underlying assets.

The danger that occurs during the day of the three witches therefore does not affect long-term investments, with the trading volume and volatility soon returning to follow the trend of the period.

The deadline forces traders to act within a given day, increasing the volume of trading within the affected markets. Many believe that triple witching causes high volatility in the underlying markets and on the same contracts expiring both in the previous week and on the day of expiration itself. In some cases this may be true, but it can also turn out to be a rather calm day.

Chapter 28 - Options and Trading

Financial options are a derivative instrument that allows us to speculate or hedge our investments on the underlying assets. For this reason we can have various forms and types of options which, in principle, we can list as follows:

- stock options
- forex options
- options on bonds
- commodity options
- ptions on cryptocurrencies
- index options
- options on ETFs

Financial options are therefore considered derivative financial instruments precisely because their price derives from the activity of the underlying as we have been able to understand so far. But where do the options arise? What are the first traces that we can find in history? Options were born in ancient Greece and were used to speculate on the olive harvest.

Use cases and features

Over time, options have been used to hedge their investments. In fact, there are options that are part of our daily life and therefore allow us to be able to secure an investment. To understand, it is good to give two examples:

- Car insurance is a put option. In fact, I am ensuring the right, but not the obligation, to redeem the insurance premium in the event that my property loses value for this or that other reason.

- The compromise for the purchase of a house is a call option. Against a premium paid, I buy the right to purchase that property on expiry, convinced that it can increase its value over time. So I block the price against the payment of a small advance that will give me the right, but not the obligation, to buy the property upon expiry of the contract.

Trading with options is the new frontier for professional traders.

A premise: today options are a financial tool that can be used to speculate on many markets, such as Forex and foreign currencies, futures, the international stock market, indexes, Bitcoin and Ethereum. The most famous and most sought after options, however, are those on the stock market.

Before going ahead, therefore, it is necessary to clarify that options are an articulated and complex tool not suitable for novice traders. This means that we are going to explain complex tools but that if used professionally they can be very profitable.

Options are investment instruments that give us the opportunity to purchase the right to buy or sell an underlying asset at a price set upon signing the contract. Then there is the sale of options that gives us the opportunity to act as an insurer, to be the dealer, and therefore to collect the premium immediately. But this also means that by selling the options I will have the obligation to buy the underlying upon expiry.

It is a bit like car insurance to go back to the previous example. If I do not suffer accidents, the insurance will collect my premium and will therefore make a profit; if, on the other hand, it will be forced to pay damages, the insurance will be lost based on the extent of the damage itself. I know it may seem like a complex and difficult tool, but we will have the opportunity to explore all these facets in the course of this precious guide.

I still want to clarify, at the cost of being repetitive, that when you buy an option you are buying a derivative, and therefore not the asset itself. Now you could say: but also CFDs are a derivative that allows us to speculate without buying or selling the underlying asset.

As you have seen, Stock Exchange Options are speculative instruments that allow you to invest in the direction of the market. With Options, however, there are also non-directional strategies that few experts in the sector are able to teach.

A key factor to consider when trading options, however, is the expiration. In fact, when we trade in options we also have to calculate the time interval within which our forecast will have to come true. In fact, with options, you don't just have to decide whether the market will go up or down. The essential factor, in fact, is to understand and predict within what time frame this will happen. Now this feature implies a further analytical study on the graph.

Two types of options

- call options
- put options

Each of these two options can be bought and

sold. We are talking about specialized and advanced market tools that use Wall Street sharks to move markets.

How does options trading work?

Please note that the tips in this guide are intended to give you the basics to start trying options trading. If you want to deepen the world of options, you will have to analyze all the concepts that I am listing in this guide with a serious trading course that lives up to expectations. Consider setting up a call with our experts to understand how to study options with the same method that is used on Wall Street.

Options trading now works like any other market trading, so there will be:

- a buyer
- a seller

However, as we have seen, options can be used to trade on all major markets. In this book, however, we will focus on seeing how options on the stock market work.

Call options

Let's take Microsoft stock as an example and suppose we want to buy a call option at the strike price of $200 with expiration in 8 weeks. This means that I am reserving the right to purchase Microsoft for $200 in two months. Now two things can happen in this case:

Microsoft's price goes up, and so I'm going to make a profit from the difference between the option price at expiry and the strike price. In short: if the option price goes from $200 to $250 by the expiration date, I will have a potential gain of 50 dollars for each share of the option. In this case, being the American stock market, each option grants us the right to as many as 100 Microsoft shares. Yes, you got it right: there are 5000 dollars of potential earnings. From these you will have to subtract the premium, which is the price you paid to open your option on the market. In this case, therefore, I have generated profit.

If I sell a call option I will collect the price of the premium, but I am selling and therefore I have an obligation to honor the circumstance of the market upon expiry. If, on the other hand, Microsoft's price goes to $150, whoever bought my put option will expire it, losing the premium that will be my actual earnings. In this case, I am playing the role of the insurer.

In summary: when I buy a Microsoft option, I expect the price to go up. Against a premium paid, therefore, I will reserve the right to exercise my option and close the option as soon as Microsoft's price rises by the deadline, thus generating a profit.

If, on the other hand, I have sold the call option, I want the price to drop to collect the premium. If I sell a call option and, upon expiration, the price will be higher, I will have to pay the difference to the buyer, and therefore I am subjected to very important risks. For this reason, options are not suitable tools for all investors.

Put options

Let's take Tesla stock as an example in this case. If I expect Tesla's value to depreciate, I will buy a put option, and then I will guarantee myself the right, but not the obligation, to sell the underlying at the strike price. Let's say you buy a put option at $400. In that case it is expected that the price will drop by the expiry date that I set myself in order to be able to generate a profit always from the 100 shares that my option covers. In that case it is selling short. Even in such a context we have two possibilities.

If I buy a put option I expect the price to range from $400 to $350. In that case, against the prize, I will collect the price difference multiplied by 100. This means that, also in this case, I have the possibility to collect a potential gain of $5000 against the premium paid. In Tesla's case, for example, the premium is about $5 per share. This means that I will have to pay a premium of 500 dollars to have, in exchange, an option that covers 100 shares. The break-even price for the trader will be given by the difference between the strike price and the sell price.

If I sell a put option I expect the price to go up, and so my goal is to collect the premium that will become my actual earnings. Unfortunately, however, it can happen that the price goes down. In that context, therefore, I will be subjecting myself to very serious risks that can seriously jeopardize my capital. This is because, upon expiry, I will have to honor my option by paying the price difference to the buyer. If, on the other hand, Tesla's price goes up, I will have collected the premium in the same way as the insurer of your car who takes your money every six months or annually.

Many beginners approaching options are tempted to sell options precisely because the premium is cashed out immediately, and is therefore a sum of money that you will immediately see available in your trading account. The problem, however, is that if the positions go against our expectations and we ignore the strategies that allow us to create hedging structures, we can really get hurt. For this reason, I would like to stress once again that options are potentially the most fascinating trading tool in the market, given its versatility, but that options trading is not child's play.

If you want to try your hand at options trading, you must necessarily consider the idea of investing in training. In fact, first it is necessary to study the functioning of the options and the creation of structures with options. You will have to learn Greek analysis and you will have to decide whether to trade directional or non-directional trading.

The basis of all options strategies

As we have seen, options are derivatives, and therefore in very rare cases the options expire. The reason is that options are mainly used to speculate from the price fluctuations of the underlying asset. However, it is good to say that not all options will follow the price of the underlying. For this reason, the price of the options may decrease over time. All of these features need to be considered before starting options trading.

Before starting to trade with options, you must necessarily understand how the Greeks work, and therefore understand and interpret these statistical facts that are used to quantify the risk that can arise from trading in options. The Greeks that must be taken into consideration are four specifically: Delta, Vega, Gamma and Theta. Now let's see in detail what these parameters measure and why they are so important for our operations.

More on the Greeks

Delta is the parameter that has the purpose of measuring the sensitivity of the option price when the price of the underlying changes. In summary, this is a parameter that shows us the number of points of displacement expected for the value of each point variation of the underlying activity. Please note that a movement point of the underlying is not always equivalent to a movement point for the option. Delta values range from 0 to 1 for Calls and from 0 to -1 for Put.

The Vega value is intended to assess the sensitivity of the option we are examining by virtue of the volatility of the chart of the underlying instrument. In technical terms, the Vega is the price value that will change on the option to respond to a 1% change in the activity of the underlying chart.

The Gamma value has the task of showing the sensitivity of the Delta value. For this reason, in technical terms, it is considered the engine of the Delta. The parameter always varies according to the changes in the price recorded in the underlying activity.

Theta has the task of measuring the decrease

in the value of the option over time. The more the option expires, it can become unprofitable. In technical terms, Theta aims to show a theoretical dollar value that the option will lose every day.

For this reason, when you decide to trade in options, you must be aware that it is a complex and risk-free activity. For this reason it will be necessary to understand the degree of risk before starting. Obviously, training on options as a tool will need to be accompanied by the study of technical analysis and fundamental analysis of the charts, especially if you choose to do directional trading with options. If, on the other hand, you are looking for less complex derivatives that always allow you to use financial leverage, you can consider the idea of trading with CFDs.

Chapter 29 - Put Options

Let's try to understand how the purchase of a put option works. Suppose we are peach growers and we want to insure ourselves against possible price changes at the time of sale. Thanks to the purchase of a put option, we have the right to sell a certain quantity of peaches (e.g. 100 quintals) at a fixed price (e.g. $70 per quintal) at a certain maturity (e.g. December 2021) . The cost of our put option is the premium (eg $1.5 per quintal). Who will collect this premium? Those who issue this option. So, by paying this premium of $150 (1.5 $x 100 q.) We buy the right to sell the apples at 70 $/q. to the counterparty that issued the option on the expiry date provided for in the contract (December 2021). At the expiration we can have this situation:

- The market price is less than $70, for example $60. We can always sell our peaches for $70;

- The market price is above $70, for example $80. We will avoid exercising the option (writing the cost of the put option in the balance sheet), selling the harvest at the market price.

We can also give an example relating to financial activities. Let's assume we have a bearish view on Microsoft stock three months from now. Today the stock is quoted at $40, but our forecast is that it can drop as low as $35 or even $25. Therefore, we decide to buy a put with a strike with a $40 strike, expiring in three months, paying a premium of $2 per share. Let's summarize our position:

- Underlying: 100 Microsoft shares
- Strike Price: $40
- Deadline: December 2021
- Prize: $2

It is clear that if we had bought the 100

Microsoft shares without using the options, our outlay would have been $4,000. With the purchase of a put, the total outlay is $200 (maximum risk). A big difference, especially from the point of view of controlling the risk of the operation.

Chapter 30 - Calls Options

In the previous chapter we discussed how put options work. Now we dive a little deeper into call options.

Let's take a practical example: suppose our business consists in buying wheat for the purpose of processing it and obtaining flour for resale.

However, unforeseen events (drought, fires, etc.) could cause a limited harvest to the point of creating the conditions for a sharp rise in prices. To avoid paying too high a price for wheat in the coming months, we could make an agreement with the farmers using a call option. We buy from the farmers the right to buy a certain quantity of wheat (e.g. 100 quintals) at a certain date (e.g. December 2021) at a very low price (e.g. $9 per quintal). That is what call options are all about. We get the right to buy wheat (underlying asset) at a fixed date (expiration date) and at a certain price (strike) by paying a certain amount (premium, e.g. $0.5 per quintal). Now let's see what can happen once the expiration date is reached (we said December 2021).

- The price of wheat increases up to $12 / q. due to a disappointing harvest. Our option is convenient for which we exercise it, by purchasing the underlying at $9;

- The price of wheat dropped to $8/ q because it was a good harvest. We do not exercise the right and we simply write the cost of the option in the balance sheet. On the other hand, the goal was to protect ourselves (hedging) from any price increases beyond $9. As you can see, our call options worked like an insurance.

Chapter 31 - Vanilla Options

In this chapter we address a particular topic that even experienced options traders often ignore: vanilla options. Never as in this case it is necessary to go down to the fundamentals to clarify the basic concepts. In fact, we are sure that if you are reading this chapter it is because you do not know what vanilla options are and therefore you do not know the advantages of options trading.

The same term "vanilla" could appear to you "exotic" but here we are not talking about unconventional currencies that often arouse so much interest in the Forex market. We are not talking about binary options either, which, as you certainly know, have been banned for some time and in any case have nothing to do with vanilla options.

After having clarified what vanilla options are not, we can now move on to their definition.

What Vanilla options are

Vanilla options have an almost exotic flavor but, in reality, there is little exotic about them. In fact, these are trading instruments through which you can get hold not of a physical asset but of a right to buy or sell an asset no later than a specific date. Since you are the owner of that right, it would be up to you to decide whether to exercise it or not.

But this definition of vanilla options closely resembles that of another speculative investment tool: futures. Well, let's clear the field of any misunderstanding by highlighting the vanilla options do not work like futures but rather have different characteristics that we will deepen in the next paragraphs.

Vanilla options and futures

There are many differences between vanilla options and futures but for convenience we report here only the main ones with the aim of clearing the field of misunderstandings.

- Futures determine the obligation to buy an asset that is the subject of the right when the date stipulated in the contract comes into effect. Vanilla options are not. By investing in this tool, in fact, you will only acquire the right to buy, but you can decide whether to exercise it or not. From this point of view, therefore, vanilla options are more flexible than futures.

- Vanilla options allow you to exercise the right even before expiration if this is convenient.

- Vanilla options have an initial premium. Therefore, to get the right to exercise the purchase or sale, you will have to pay a premium that is not related to price fluctuations. The comparison with futures does not arise precisely because there is no premium when choosing the latter.

In light of the elements indicated above,

vanilla options are configured as a valid tool for protecting one's capital.

How vanilla options work

After specifying what vanilla options are, we can now move on to analyze how they work. The procedure is as follows.

If you want to own an option, you will have to pay the seller a premium of a defined amount. This premium is not determined by chance but by a series of elements such as the current strike price or the price of the instrument.

If you buy an option you will have to pay the premium if you sell an option instead you will receive it.

How does the negotiation mechanism work in the future? The procedure is simple. The date by which you have the right to exercise the option is called the expiry date. Options that have a longer maturity typically have higher premiums than vanillas with a shorter maturity. Perhaps this principle reminds you of insurance and in fact you are not wrong this time because the vanilla options premium works in a similar way.

Determining the premium

How is the premium determined? Among the many factors influencing this parameter, the volatility of the underlying asset is among the most important.

It goes like this. With higher volatility, the option price rises. Conversely, the price falls if the volatility falls. The increase in price with greater volatility is explained in light of the possibility of a larger market movement occurring which can lead to even greater profits.

You can generally decide to close the option when you want to make the most of the movement and thus obtain a more interesting profit.

Vanilla options trading

And here we are at the heart of the guide: how to trade vanilla options. Keep in mind everything we said above but change the general context.

Vanilla options can be used not only as a defense tool against too strong price fluctuations but also as a means of speculation.

When you buy a put or call option you will have to immediately pay a premium of the cash balance of the account but the gains you can have are unlimited. However, when you go to sell the options, you receive a reward by crediting the account's liquid balance. However, you will have an exposure to losses that could be unlimited which would be triggered in the event that the market were to move against you.

To limit this risk you can use stop orders on options.

If you buy options, you run a limited risk as the maximum amount you can lose is equal to the premium. By selling vanilla options you can generate a large profit as you offer third party protection on that position.

Concretely, the first move to make in options trading is to predict the market trend for a certain asset. If you believe that this asset will increase in price, you have three choices:

- buy the asset through traditional CFD trading (spot position)
- buy a call option
- buy a put option

Advantages of trading options

After having clarified how to trade on Vanilla options, we can now have some more elements to understand what are the advantages of this investment tool. There are many but the most important are these three.

- It is a safe investment. Trading options is less risky than trading the underlying asset.

- Options express offer a complete view of the market. In fact, you can combine long and short call and put options with long or short spot positions.

- Unlike spot trading, where you can only speculate upwards or downwards, with options you can execute a strategy based on different factors (time horizon, market trend, difference between the current strike price and the asset price)

Are vanilla options good for new traders?

Vanilla options have no additional risks compared to CFD Trading.

This also applies to novice traders. For some investors, options aren't quite the best to start with, but they can be safely used to speculate if you understand what their risk profile is.

I encourage you to study the topic very well before placing your first trade.

Chapter 32 - Barrier Options

Barrier options are a very interesting tool offered by different brokers.

Barrier options are part of the exotic options category, so they are neither binary options nor American options. The main peculiarity of this type of option is the presence of the barrier, which in case of achievement would put an end to the option itself. Although now the topic may seem difficult to understand, do not worry because everything will be clearer by reading this chapter.

There is no stamp duty on the barrier options, while there is coverage of the negative balance. This means that the trader will not be able to go into debt with the broker and will not be able to lose more than their available balance.

We specify that this chapter does not

constitute investment advice, but is intended as a guide for those who want to learn about barrier options. So consider this chapter as a simple help to get to know this tool better.

Let's start by saying that we are talking about derivative financial products that have the particularity of the barrier, as already mentioned.

Having understood the meaning of the underlying asset, we can proceed with the explanation of the barrier options. In fact, as we have already explained, the barrier is the extra factor of this financial product. Should the price of the underlying reach the predetermined barrier, which is called a knock-out, the position will automatically close at a loss or profit, depending on the direction of the market price of the underlying.

It is a very similar concept, but definitely not the same, to the stop loss and the take profit.

We talked about the exit barrier, that is the knock-out, but in reality there is also an entry barrier, called the knock-in. This can be useful because you can't always be in front of the monitor checking prices. Automated trading in this sense is a great help for traders.

How they work

We now come to the explanation of how barrier options work. First of all, it is essential to specify that the barrier options can only be opened with the purchase and not with the sale, unlike other types of options such as vanilla options.

In any case, the possibility of trading is bi-directional, in fact we can open:

- a call option if we want to invest in the rise in the price of the underlying asset
- a put option if instead we want to invest in the fall in the price of the underlying asset

Is there leverage on barrier options? The

answer is yes, so consider that your investment can multiply and this can be a double-edged sword, since not only will the gains increase, but also the losses.

Regarding the expiration, we remind you that the duration of the barrier options tends to vary from 6 to 12 months from the opening of the positions. However, if the price of the underlying should previously reach the knock-out price, the position will close automatically, as already explained. Furthermore, if you intend to manually close an option with a barrier before its expiry, you can do it whenever you want.

Let's talk now about the costs related to barrier options. The opening price is determined by the difference between the selling price of the underlying and the knock-out selected by the trader plus a premium to be paid to the broker.

Furthermore, we specify that depending on the your choice, the situation changes accordingly:

Call option = (selling price of the underlying asset - knock-out level) + knock-out premium.

Put option = (knock-out level - selling price of the underlying asset) + knock-out premium.

It is also necessary to consider the size of the position you want to open, or the number of contracts you want to buy.

With regard to the premium, it should be added that it must be paid in full when an option with a barrier is opened, but will be returned if the position is closed before the knock-out threshold is reached. What determines the knock-out price? Essentially it comes from the volatility of the market you want to invest in.

There is also a commission to be paid at the opening and closing of each barrier option, usually equal to 0.1 currency contract units per lot. Finally, a final cost to consider is that of overnight financing, should the position be open for more than one day. The latter is a cost also present in CFD trading.

Chapter 33 - Binary Options

Binary options are a type of investment with which anyone can profit from the change in value of commodities, stocks, various assets and even the Forex market.

The reason binary options have become so popular in recent years is because investors only have to choose one thing in order to invest. To invest in binary options, the trader must make a decision between "yes" and "no", which in the world of binary options are called the "put" option and the "call" option.

If, for example, you want to invest in gold, you don't necessarily have to buy the asset. If you use binary options, you just decide whether, in your opinion, the price of gold will go up or down in a given period of time.

One of the main advantages of investing in binary options is that you can also choose the period within which, in your opinion, the price of gold will rise or fall. These time frames range from 60 seconds to one month. You can simply say: in my opinion, the price of gold will have dropped in the next 60 seconds.

To make this investment serious and profitable, of course, we need to use effective binary options strategies and know the dynamics of binary options trading very well.

For this reason, in this chapter we explain in detail everything you need to know before starting to invest through binary options and all the information that is always useful to know, even for experienced traders.

Binary options, we repeat, are a simple way to invest and earn if you are faithful to a correct strategy.

The gain from investing in binary options is given by a previously established profit if the option goes "in the money". On the other hand, the profit is zero if the binary option ends "out of the money", or if your forecast turned out to be wrong.

A binary option is executed automatically, which means that those who invest in binary options do not have to decide whether to buy or sell a particular asset.

How binary options work

Investors are particularly attracted to investing in binary options due to their apparent simplicity, especially since the investor only has to decide if something will happen or not.

For example, a binary option could simply be composed of the question: "Do you think the price of ABC shares will be higher than 25 dollars on November 22nd at 10:45 am?". If the price is 27 dollars on the day and at the specified time, whoever opened the binary option automatically receives a profit for having "guessed" the answer.

Yes, binary options are a very easy way to make money on market fluctuations, but traders need to know what the risks and benefits of this heavily criticized tool are.

Binary options are different from traditional options. The latter have different payouts, commissions and risks, not to mention a profoundly different liquidity structure. For speculation or hedging operations, binary options can be an alternative, but only if the trader fully understands the two possible outcomes of these "exotic options".

Binary options are classified as "exotic options", but they are extremely simple to use. The most common binary option is a "high-low" option. With access to the stocks, indexes, commodities and Forex markets, "high-low" binary options are also called fixed return options, because the option has an expiration date.

If a trader bets correctly on the direction of the market and the price at the time of expiry is on the correct side of the strike price, the trader is paid a fixed return regardless of how much the price of the instrument has moved. A trader who bets incorrectly on the direction of the market loses their investment in full.

The strike price

In the binary options market, the strike price or exercise price is the price at which an option is purchased.

Types of binary options

There are various types of binary options through which to invest and earn. All types of binary options never involve buying or selling an asset, but they do provide a forecast by the trader, who must be able to guess the direction of the price over time in order to make money from binary options trading.

Here is the list of the various types of binary options that investors can trade and make money from.

High/Low Binary Options

They are the typical binary options also called Call/Put. They are the simplest to use. We are talking about contracts for which, if we think that the price will rise with respect to the current price and over a certain period of time, we will open a call option. If, on the other hand, we believe that the asset price will decrease, we will open a Put option. We remind you that the expiry time is chosen directly by the trader.

With the arrival of the deadline, the trader will be in the money if they have guessed the direction of the trend and therefore if they have bet on a correct forecast, and will be out of the money if they are wrong.

Then there is the condition in which the closing price of the binary option is the same as that of the opening: in this case it is at the money and the broker returns the entire amount of the bet.

The investment profit on High/Low binary options is at a fixed percentage, which means that the trader already knows how much they will be able to earn before opening the order - generally around 80% of the invested capital.

60 seconds binary options

This type of binary options expires exactly after 60 seconds and is the type of options most loved by traders. The main advantage of 60-second binary options is that if the price is clearly moving in a certain direction, the trader can take advantage and trigger several consecutive 60-second binary options orders and maximize profits.

It is ideal for those traders who are looking for quick profits and are, in turn, quick in identifying market movements.

Touch Binary Options

Touch binary options are another way to trade options.

Through a touch option, you bet on the fact that the price of an asset touches or does not touch a certain price.

Instead of predicting whether the price of the underlying asset will rise or fall, the touch binary options trader must bet on whether a certain level will be touched or not.

This level can be both higher and lower than the current price of the asset.

Touch Binary Options can only be opened on weekends when the markets are closed. Then, they are valid for all the following 5 days, or for the 5 trading days that go from Monday to Friday.

If an asset touches or exceeds the level previously specified by the Broker on Monday afternoon, the broker declares the win and the trader receives their profit which can even reach 500% of the stake. If you are out of the money on Monday, the position will still remain open until Friday, and the platform continues to check daily to see if the price has reached the level necessary to make the Touch position a winner.

One Touch binary options are ideal for those traders who think that the price of an underlying asset will reach a certain level in the future, but are not sure how long-lasting the trend can be.

Through no-Touch binary options, the trader wins when the price of the asset for the entire period never reaches the level specified by the Broker.

Range binary options

Range binary options offer very high payouts and are available on all major broker platforms. Within this type of options, the trader must predict what will be the movements of the asset on which they have decided to bet on. The broker indicates the range, that is the highest price and the lowest price on an asset, the trader must identify if the price will fluctuate within the indicated range or if it will go beyond, both down and up.

The gain in the binary options market depends on the following:

- the amount invested;
- the profit of the trade.

The invested amount is the money that the trader uses to purchase the contract. The trader is free to decide the amount that they will use for the purchase of the contract. However, it is always advisable to use good risk management by not risking too much in a trade.

Payments are sometimes determined automatically by brokers. However, some platforms will adjust the payment based on the trade expiration date, the expected profits of the trade and the level of difficulty linked to the possibility of the contract to reach the goal, according to the trader's settings.

This is a brief summary of how binary options work. If you've read this lesson, you should be able to understand how the market works and use it to your advantage.

If a trader believes that the market will go up, they must buy a "call" binary option. If the trader believes that the market will go down, they will have to open a "put" position. In the case of a call option, in order to make money the price must be above the strike price at the time of expiry.

To make money with a binary put option, the price must be below the strike price at the time of expiry. The strike price, expiration date, payout potential and risk are all factors disclosed prior to the purchase of binary options.

For most high-low binary options, the strike

price is the current price or rate of the underlying asset of a financial instrument, such as the SP 500 index, the euro-dollar exchange rate (EUR/USD) or a stock. Therefore, the trader simply has to bet whether the future price at the expiration of the binary option will be higher or lower than the current price.

Some people think that binary options are like gambling. However, if you use longer time frames, like weekly or monthly binary options, you can actually implement all the trading and analysis strategies in this book.

Chapter 34 - Turbo Options

Turbo options are those binary options whose expiration ranges from 15 seconds to 5 minutes. Like any other short-term bet, the hidden risk is much more but they are also relatively "fun" for customers looking for entertainment rather than real trading opportunities. Please, be aware that turbo options are pure speculation, something a trader should avoid at all costs.

What turbo options are

In a nutshell, turbo options encompass all types of binary options with short term expiry. In their fastest form, they last only 15 seconds.

The turbo options get their name from the fact that they are traded with a very short expiration, which makes everything very adrenaline.

The main bases of binary options remain the same: you have to indicate and focus on which direction the price of the underlying will take, up (call) or down (put).

Anyone who has analyzed charts in a short period of time knows that even in a single minute everything can change and the movements are mostly unpredictable.

Binary options predictions are complicated and standard indicators in most cases do not help, as the analysis timeframes are extremely short.

On the technical front, turbo options need a constant flow of updates on the price (so as to have a certain price when the option is opened and another at the exact time for expiration). Not all instruments have enough liquidity to make this scenario possible, which is why turbo options are only active on the most popular currencies, stocks and commodities.

Trading or gambling?

There are those who believe that turbo options are based on luck and are like roulette. We are of this opinion.

Opening the position involves a very simple task, selecting one of the two possible outcomes (such as red or black in roulette) and waiting for the ball to stop. It is quick and easy and there is no need for prolonged decision making. There is the power of probabilities, of the calculation of sequences and of luck, but nothing else.

The criterion for which we can still talk about trading falls on the premise that the result is derived from a market action. A miniaturized version of the markets has its own specific quirks that need to be learned. But just like in trading, you can take advantage of mini-trends, reversals or support or resistance levels.

But turbo options aren't new of their kind. Also called "tick trading" or "static trading", fast trading attracts investors but the numbers are relatively small. This is because it requires larger amounts of capital to maintain margin and is perceived as a greater risk that does not respect any kind of fundamental analysis.

We warmly advise you to stay away from turbo options.

Chapter 35 - 10 Steps to Start Trading Options

Options are an alternative way of making money on the stock markets, Forex or through commodities. As anticipated, one of the main benefits of trading options is that you don't have to buy stocks, commodities and currencies for real.

If trading with options online has aroused interest and curiosity in you but you still don't understand how to invest, here is a simple and immediate guide on how to invest in options in 10 steps.

Choose the underlying asset

The first decision you need to make when opening any type of options position is to figure out which asset, commodity or stock you want to bet on.

Once you have chosen which type of

instrument to open your options, it is time to decide whether to go long or short. Namely: do you think the instrument you have chosen will increase in price? Or will the price go down?

If you think that the value, for example of oil, will fall in a given period of time then you will open a put option, otherwise - if you think the price will rise - you will have to bet on a call option.

Choose a broker

You need a broker to trade options, for this reason it is necessary to choose your broker well. Every options broker offers various types of trading accounts, giving you the opportunity to open an account that can give you maximum benefits and many extras depending on the volume of the position you choose to open to make money with options.

Choose the expiration date

Once you have defined the type of instrument to use as the basis for your options investment and once you have chosen the broker that is perfect for you, it is time to choose the expiry date of your position as well.

It is essential to choose the expiry date that you prefer and that best suits your options strategy, as there are many events that can affect the price of a financial instrument every day.

Calculate and compare the potential profit

When you are about to open a position, it is good to do some research and understand if you are receiving an affordable potential profit. Each broker independently defines the profit for a successful options investment, so you need to do a research and find out if there are any other brokers that offer a higher profit. In this way, with the same investment, you will earn more money thanks to options.

This is a factor to always consider when trading options, since the profit you get from your positions can vary from one broker to another. The advice is to check your potential profit on the investment you are about to make in options through various brokers; comparing the potential profit between the various brokers will allow you to easily find out which, at a given moment, is offering the best earning opportunity.

Discover the hottest trends

After studying to understand which asset and which maturity to choose, you must make sure that you are using all the tools at your disposal to make money through options, so that your position is a winner.

Many brokers offer the latest financial news on the trading platform, and others also show which options positions are hottest at any given time among investors around the world.

The best options brokers always show what trending options positions there are, so it will be very easy to see which bet is attracting the most volumes, i.e. the one that is believed to be a winner by many investors.

Increase your trading budget

Competition between options brokers is certainly a factor that every trader should always take into consideration. For this reason, there is always some new convenient offer to increase your trading budget.

Welcome bonuses attract a lot of interest among traders, but there are also other loyalty bonuses offered by binary options brokers.

Therefore, always check if you are eligible to receive a trading bonus through your broker, especially before opening a position with your money.

Always be ready

You can't always know in advance when an unmissable options trading opportunity will arise, and that's a factor to keep in mind. Thus, it is always recommended to have access to both the trading platform on your computer and on your smartphone when signing up with the options broker of your choice.

Cover your trades

Many traders are looking for a chance to hedge their open position on the options market. A very simple way to do this is to use multiple trading accounts on different brokers and take advantage of the welcome bonuses, using them to open other positions and thus cover any losses.

Take advantage of the Roll Forward order

The Roll Forward is a new order that has recently been made available by most options brokers. This is available only after opening a trade and offers the possibility to extend the expiration of the option where you have invested. The expiration will be postponed and the new expiration of your options position will automatically become the earliest available.

The power of early closure

While many traders will be more than prepared to wait until the expiration date is reached, if an extraordinary event occurs that pushes the price of the asset you have chosen in the opposite direction from what you thought, you can consider using the "early exit" order.

Many brokers offer the option to close the option on which you have invested before its expiry. You will have to pay a penalty for early closure but in this way you will be able to limit your losses.

Chapter 36 - Advanced Trading Strategies

In which direction can the market move? The answer is: up, down and sideways. Traders often forget about the latter option. There are infinite assets that do not move in clear terms, and after a period of observation they remain more or less in the same place where they started. This applies to every time frame.

Selling secured call options

In general, the strategy is suitable for all base values where there are liquid options. In this chapter we will take a look from the perspective of a shareholder. Requirements: the shareholder must have 100 shares of a base value or a multiple of these. They can only carry out a covered trade where they sell a call option for 100 shares in their portfolio. For this, they receive the bonus option. As the call rules specify, they are obliged to deliver 100 shares at the purchase price of the option if the buyer so wishes and no matter what higher price the market may give.

If the price of the securities increases strongly, the holder of the option in fact avails themselves of their right to exercise the option. The seller of the option must therefore sell their securities at the fixed purchase price. This call is covered because whoever sells the option actually owns the stocks related to the call in a deposit: they can therefore fulfill their obligation deriving from the options contract at any time.

There is no risk for this trade. The main disadvantage of the position is the possibility of missing out on big winnings. Instead, it increases the likelihood of smaller wins. And another important thing: in terms of price weakness of the base value, the seller of the covered call is never in a worse position than the owner of the securities. If the market moves sideways, the option seller profits from the gradual decline in value of the option over time.

The bonus received on a regular basis is called an extra dividend by some people. Of course this is not a dividend, but it is still an additional source of income that can be collected every month.

Offensive and defensive variations

With the choice of the short call, there is the possibility of modeling the trade in a more offensive or defensive way. If you want to concede an upward move, the strike should be further out of the money. The downside is that the value of the time earned is smaller. If the base value has a predisposition for weakness, the position can easily lose money. On the other hand, you can receive many bonuses of value over time with a strike at the money or even in the money, but you have to give up a clear profit by moving up the base value from the beginning.

It is a good idea to use elements of technical

analysis as a support. A simple system is to illustrate two moving averages (MA). For example the MA (9) and the MA (18). If the MA (9) is above the MA (18), the base value shifts towards the other. The short call strike should be out of the money.

Ideally, we orientate ourselves on the trend existing in the base value. Graphic indicators such as the Convergence / Divergence of the Moving Average (MACD) or the use of three MAs can also be useful. Technical analysts can be creative here, but even simple systems get the job done.

Where is the trick?

There is a scenario for every trading strategy in which it does not perform well. In the case of Covered Call Options it is an oscillatory movement of the base value that allows us to take part in the profit only in small quantities, but in large quantities when it comes to losses for a subsequent retention period. This back and forth movement of the market is also called whipsaw.

It can occur if you sell a call close to the in-the-money value. As soon as the base value recovers, the short call costs a lot and the base value will practically no longer participate in the profit. If we get close to forfeiture we can either buy back the call at a higher price or let it be exercised. In this case the securities are bought from us at the market price (as the strike price is lower than the stock price). This way we can lose a lot of profits. If we buy 100 shares of the stock again and eventually sell an at-the-money call with a slight decline thereafter, the stock can drop significantly. We improve our situation a little with respect to the shareholder, but in the event of clear price losses, our loss is also very significant. Overall this would be a combination of low profits and big losses. It's unpleasant, but it can happen.

Entry point

You can choose a base value on which you can trade calmly, which ideally is a flat upward swing. If possible, take a look at the "trend context" at the time of entry: take the last two tops of the process in order to define an upward trend line.

Sell one call for every 100 shares you own that is out of the money and with a duration of 6 to 12 weeks. The lowest price that must be reached for the option premium received should be a base value of 0.8%. If the base value is a single security, the forfeiture of the option should not occur immediately after the expiry of the quarterly earnings.

Rolling and balance

Roll the contract only if it is worth 30% of the sale price. The new contract to be sold will have the longest execution time, so you can win additional bonuses. If the base value shows weakness, you will still go through a maximum of one or two strikes with the new contract.

This avoids establishing systematic losses via whipsaw. If the contract is slightly in the money, do a roll to collect even more money. This means that you acquire at least as many bonuses for the new sold contract as are necessary for the old repurchase. For this, you can choose a lead time of up to four months. With a sharp increase in the base value it is sometimes not possible to respect these terms as our call is too far in the money, but it can be useful to balance all positions including stocks and profit.

In alternative, you can buy back only the call and keep the stocks. But one must consider making a loss though. If the stock falls later you get the worst of both scenarios: a new loss of profits from the positions of the securities plus the losses for the option position. This can only be avoided with good market timing.

Useful base values

Option trades are only useful when there are liquid options at base value. In Germany these are only the largest capitalization companies in the DAX. In the US, there are around 150 stocks with good stock options markets.

Tip: Take a look at the stocks in the S&P 100 index. This lesser known index is a subset of the S&P 500 and contains the 100 largest US stocks. The drawbacks of stocks, especially in combination with trades of all kinds over several weeks, are the occasional jump in prices in both directions following the announcement of the quarterly figures. In particular, beginners may be interested in the ETF (Exchange Traded Funds) sector which is traded in the United States, which partly has very liquid options. This especially applies to ETFs marketed under the SPDR brand. The iShares brand fund options are also mentioned for completeness. With ETFs, there are no risks associated with quarterly earnings.

In general they should be slow but steady rising stocks. With stocks rising sharply it often makes more sense to simply hold onto the stock. But how do things work with falling stocks? In general, stocks that fail to advance in price should not be kept in the portfolio. Even the covered call strategy does not change this situation.

Maintenance and exercise of the option

If you keep the option until it expires, there are two possible scenarios: if it is out of the money it means that if exercising it would not be efficient, you realize the bonus earned as a profit without doing anything else. If the option is in the money, however, it will be exercised upon forfeiture. The seller of the call has their securities bought at a strike price, lower than the market price in this case, and the call is removed from the portfolio. The position (option and stock) is therefore almost always closed in profit through the balance. A scenario that occurs occasionally is an early exercise of the option on the date of dividends. If the expected dividend payment is not high enough, it may be worthwhile for those who buy the option to exercise the options before the expiry date.

Chapter 37 - Combining Options

Combinations of options are strategies composed of calls and puts in different proportions with which you can receive benefits from different results and events. When you buy a stock for speculative purposes, at the time of the sale you receive positive returns if the stock price has risen and negative returns if the price has fallen, therefore in a linear fashion. With the combinations of call and put options you can benefit from different situations, growth or decrease.

In fact, these combinations expand the chances of earning profits. For example, it is possible to construct a portfolio that has positive returns based on the simple deviation of the price of the underlying from the current state, without choosing a precise direction. To achieve this goal, it is necessary to compose portfolios of options, both buy and sell, which combine the various profit profiles of the individual derivative instruments.

We talk about the deviation of the price of the underlying from the current state, but it is more precise to refer to an exercise price which will be the reference value of the combinations. Since these are simultaneous positions on call and put options, the combinations require that the strike price is close to the price practiced by the market at the current time. If this were not the case, one of the two positions would be very expensive.

How options combinations work

Although combining different profit profiles facilitates the achievement of the goals of the trader, using combinations of options is not an exercise without cost or risk. In each of the possible modular portfolios, as in the rest of financial transactions, there is a strict rule that imposes a trade-off, a choice: high profits or low level of risk.

The risk attitude of traders determines a

different choice regarding the trade-off just mentioned, conditioning the constitution of different combinations. Once again, the level of risk aversion and expectations of market trends guide the choice of investments to be made.

In the combinations considered in the next chapters, it must be assumed that only options that have a share as underlying are used, but the strategies could be applied to any financial instrument that can be traded on the markets. Let's get started!

CPSIA information can be obtained
at www.ICGtesting.com
Printed in the USA
LVHW081151241122
733912LV00015B/672

9 781806 211128